IT'S A GIRL

WOMEN WRITERS ON
RAISING DAUGHTERS

EDITED BY ANDREA J. BUCHANAN

SEAL PRESS

IT'S A GIRL:
WOMEN WRITERS ON RAISING DAUGHTERS

Amy Bloom's "Me and My Girls" was originally published in *New Woman* magazine in 1995.

Jennifer Lauck's "Links" is reprinted from *Show Me the Way: A Memoir in Stories*, originally published by Atria in 2004.

Published by
Seal Press
An Imprint of Avalon Publishing Group, Incorporated
1400 65th Street, Suite 250
Emeryville, CA 94608

ISBN-13: 978-1-58005-147-7
ISBN-10: 1-58005-147-2

9 8 7 6 5 4 3 2 1

Library of Congress Cataloging-in-Publication Data

It's a girl; women writers on raising daughters / edited by Andrea J. Buchanan.
  p. cm.
 ISBN-13: 978-1-58005-147-7
 ISBN-10: 1-58005-147-2
 1. Girls. 2. Mothers and daughters. 3. Parenting. I. Buchanan, Andrea J.
HQ777.I8 2006
306.874'3—dc22
 2005030345

Cover design by Gia Giasullo, studio eg
Interior design by Domini Dragoone
Printed in Canada by Transcontinental
Distributed by Publishers Group West

To Emi,
my sweet girl.

CONTENTS

SHINING, SHIMMERING, SPLENDID

ON BEAUTY AND A DAUGHTER

GARDEN CITY

PASSING IT ON

Introduction

When I was pregnant with my daughter, I was thrilled to be expecting a girl. Other people, though, were concerned. "Is your husband okay with that?" they asked. "Don't worry," they reassured me, "you can try again." Some even gave me tight-lipped tsks of warning. "Girls are tough," they said. Others were happy for me, visions of flouncing pink dresses and promises of mother–daughter bonding evidently overtaking any urge they might have had to dispense admonitions.

My own feelings lay somewhere between the two extremes. My husband was fine with having a girl, I wasn't worried about needing to try again for a boy, I outright disbelieved the rumor that girls were harder to raise, and pink held no particular allure for me.

Mother–daughter bonding, though—that was a potential stumbling block. Having a girl felt natural to me, but I'd be lying if I said I didn't worry just the slightest that our relationship might be unavoidably, inescapably fraught—less the stuff of happy shopping trips and more the stuff of door-slamming dramafests. Still, I felt confident that even if some of the mother–daughter territory might be treacherous, at least it would be familiar.

1

When I was pregnant with my son, I was decidedly more ambivalent. After the baby's male status was revealed at the ultrasound, it took me a few weeks to wrap my head around the fact that I had a boy baby inside me; that I would soon be a mother not to two sisters, but to a girl and a boy. This time the strangers were uniformly ecstatic.

"You must be so happy!" As though I wouldn't be if I were carrying a girl. Or, "Your husband must be proud!" As if he'd be disappointed to have another daughter. Countless people told me how easy boys are; how loving, how sweet, how special, how different from girls—often, and appallingly, right in front of my three-year-old daughter.

This prompted me to further investigate the "it's a boy" / "it's a girl" divide. I spoke and exchanged emails with other mothers and writers about mothering boys and girls, and I asked the following questions: Are there real differences between mothering a son and mothering a daughter? Are the ideas we have about boys and girls based on genuine differences between them, or do our ideas about their differences inform their behavior? Do boys truly love their mothers differently? Are girls really "difficult"? Are boys really "easy"? Do these stereotypes about boy and girl babies change in toddlerhood? Adolescence?

The conversation this sparked inspired me to embark on two essay collections about mothering boys and mothering girls—not instructional tomes or guidebooks, but literary explorations of what it means to mother sons and daughters, and of the differences between girls and boys. This book and its companion piece, *It's a Boy: Women Writers on Raising Sons*, published in 2005, are the result.

Like It's a Boy, the essays in It's a Girl are grouped into four sections, with each section's title coming from one of the essays in that group. The first section is Shining, Shimmering, Splendid, referencing an essay that takes it title from lyrics to the Disney princess song "A Whole New World." In this section, writers confront the new world of being a mother to a daughter instead of a daughter to a mother, working out the various messages of feminism, princess power, and what makes a girl a girl. The second section, On Beauty and a Daughter, features frank writing on body image, eating disorders, plastic surgery, and the cultural—and maternal—expectations of feminine beauty. The third section, Garden City, examines both the complicated joy of mother–daughter bonding and the somewhat darker notion of girl-mothering as a way to heal wounds from the past. The final section, Passing it On, is about letting go, and about the ongoing dance of cleaving and separation between mothers and daughters.

In Shining, Shimmering, Splendid, eight writers discuss their ambivalence about what one essayist calls "contemporary American girldom." The world of girls—in the pinkest, sparkliest, most princessy sense of the word—is largely foreign for these mothers, most of them self-identified feminists, products of the changing cultural landscape of the '70s and '80s. Many of these writers chafe at the restrictions they feel are placed on them due to gender and wonder how they can raise a girl when they are so conflicted themselves. In "Her Perfect Woman," Carolyn Alessio suspects that her true calling might not be as a mother, but as a 1950s husband—the kind who stays late at the office and returns home after drinks with friends just in time to catch a glimpse of the baby before bedtime. Kim Fischer, a mother of triplets, discovers the power of princesses when her three girls succumb to the siren song of Disney characters in "Shining, Shimmering, Splendid." In "Ladylike," Gabrielle Smith-Dluha is dismayed that her five-year-old girl might be destined to forever be a rap-loving tomboy, thanks to her two older brothers and her mother's lack of feminine wiles. Rebecca Steinitz ("Tough Girls") admits to "unabashed brainwashing" about the power and potential of girls in the course of raising her two "hard-core minifeminists," and novelist Jacquelyn Mitchard traces her evolution from boy-mother to girl-mother as she embraces her new daughter, and her own feminine side, in "Confessions of a Tomboy Mom." Yvonne Latty writes about living in a "Girl House," with an all-girl family that includes two moms, and how the girly daughter she never expected has given her a second shot at girlhood herself. Author Miriam Peskowitz ("Cheerleader") confronts the fact that at six years old, her daughter seems to be embracing the role of girl as cheerleader—a role that women of her mother's generation worked so hard to subvert. Finally, Martha Brockenbrough, in "It's a Girl," explores her own ambivalence about being female and reveals what becoming the mother of two girls has shown her about self-acceptance and gender.

In the second section, *On Beauty and a Daughter*, six writers investigate the power of beauty, and the complicated, ultimately subjective nature of being a beautiful girl. Jenny Block's "On Being Barbie," a piece about the author's experience with multiple plastic surgeries, questions whether a mother who takes inordinate pride in her appearance can effectively impart to her daughter the lesson that beauty comes from within. In "The Food Rules," Canadian parenting author Ann Douglas discovers her teenage daughter's eating disorder and wonders what role her own focus on weight loss might play in it. Novelist Gwendolen Gross ("Feeling Is First: On Beauty and a Daughter") is more surprised by her daughter's empathy than her striking beauty, and ponders whether that combination of beauty and compassion will serve her girl or make her more vulnerable. In "Breasts: A Collage," Rachel Hall writes of her own memories of budding womanhood, contrasting that with her mother's breast cancer and her daughter's own journey toward puberty. Novelist Joyce Maynard is frank about the inescapable maternal pride and prejudice of having a beautiful baby in "The World's Most Beautiful Baby—Take Two." And Catherine Newman comes right out with the F-word—*fat*—in her essay "Baby Fat," about the surprising reaction of strangers to her baby girl's plumpness, and her own reaction to the postpartum plenitude of her own body.

In the third section, *Garden City*, nine writers explore the sometimes uneasy bond between mothers and daughters. Amy Bloom's "Me and My Girls," a celebration of mother–daughter closeness, contemplates the ways in which Bloom and her two daughters are both formed and informed by each other. In "Girl Talk," Suzanne Kamata faces a mother–daughter communication gap of the most literal sort as she learns of her daughter's deafness. Vicky Mlyniec writes about what she learned from the daughter she never had in "Daughter Dread," and Jennifer Margulis ("Spilled Wine"), who vowed to have daughters and to love them in a way she felt her mother could not love her, is surprised to find herself with a daughter who seems difficult to love. In "Garden City," Jessica Berger Gross reminisces about the complicated relationship she had with her mother and describes how she longs both for a daughter and for the chance to make things right. Kelly H. Johnson ("Park-Bench Epiphany") confronts her own childhood demons as she takes her three-year-old daughter to a playground for the very first time, and Emily Alexander Strong wants her daughter to be "A Strong Baby Girl" but realizes that instead, she is a sensitive girl who wears her mother's heart on her sleeve. In "Links," author Jennifer Lauck writes about the night she gave birth to her daughter—and made peace with the birth mother who gave her away. And in "On Wanting a Girl," Shari MacDonald Strong desperately wants a girl, and eventually has one, though not in the way she anticipated.

Finally, the seven essays in Passing It On consider the need of daughters to both bond with and separate from their mothers. In "Zen Mind, Daughter's Mind," novelist Gayle Brandeis hopes her daughter's newfound interest in Buddhism will make them grow closer, but instead it turns out to be a Zen exercise in letting go. Jill Siler's "Twenty Minutes" follows a mother and daughter on their morning commute, the mother wishing they could play hooky together even as she waves goodbye. Barbara Card Atkinson writes in "Isolation" about being nostalgic for the "claustrophobia" of life with a newborn as her preteen daughter begins the inevitable drift into adulthood, while Jody Mace looks forward to the mystery of her future teenage daughter in "Time Capsule." Novelist Katherine Weber confronts the curious odd-man-out feeling she experiences observing her girls and her husband "immersed in their father–daughter intensities" in "The Boy We Didn't Have," and in "Learning to Write," I attempt to decipher the messages my five-year-old daughter painstakingly spells out for me as she stakes out her own space. Finally, in the last essay, "Passing It On," novelist Leslie Leyland Fields ponders the maternal legacy she leaves her daughter as her teenage girl, on the cusp of adulthood, stands in the stern of an Alaskan fishing boat and learns not how to become a woman, but how to become a man.

Working on It's a Girl after completing It's a Boy was an interesting project. I began these anthologies in much the same way I approached parenting my daughter and son: with the notion that the two would be quite similar, and that any differences that might emerge could most likely be ascribed to stereotypical gender bias. Instead, just as my children have revealed themselves to be distinctly different from one another in multitudinous ways—some, undeniably, accounted for by gender, but some not—so have these books proven to have distinct themes that I didn't necessarily expect.

My initial questions about boys and girls turned out not to have definitive answers—after reading hundreds of submissions on parenting sons and daughters, I still can't tell if girls are more "complicated" or boys more prone to violence. But I can tell you something about the difference between mothers of girls and mothers of boys. For both books, I received many essay submissions from writers who were conflicted about the sex of their baby. But the concerns of writers in It's a Boy were about the otherness of the male gender: What the heck do you do with a boy? It's a Girl writers ask the same question about their daughters, but what prompts it is not fear of the unknown, but fear of what they know all too well.

Mothering a girl, according to these writers, makes a woman face herself anew, reliving her own experiences growing up as a girl. The mother of a girl must plumb the depths of the girlhood she'd thought she had safely escaped—but this time through the eyes of her daughter, whose experience is necessarily different. The pain and joy of this reliving, the merging of mother and daughter experience, and the bittersweet, inevitable separation between the two, is at the core of mothering a girl—and at the heart of the essays that make up this book.

ANDREA J. BUCHANAN
November, 2005
Philadelphia, Pennsylvania

SHINING, SHIMMERING, SPLENDID

Her Perfect Woman

CAROLYN
ALESSIO

A few days after I gave birth to my daughter, I realized my life's true calling: to be a 1950s father and husband. I would excel at the role, remaining late at the office to add detail and flourishes to my work, perhaps joining colleagues for drinks on the way home, or possibly calling my spouse to mention that I was bringing along last-minute dinner guests. Every night I would make sure, however, to be home in time to cuddle my drowsy, freshly bathed infant.

During my maternity leave, or "eternity leave," as I privately dubbed it, I quickly discovered that I was terrified of caring for my infant daughter. Charlotte was lovely, healthy, and alert, but I could not shake my trepidation and anxiety. It began when I lay shivering in post-op, bone-cold from the anesthesia for my cesarean. A nurse offered to place my newborn in my arms. "No," I said, my teeth chattering; "I'd drop her."

Once we were home, sleep deprivation probably had a lot to do with my first difficult months as a mother, but I was also daunted by one simple fact that my daughter could do nothing about: She was a girl.

Friends called me a bad feminist when I confided that I was hoping for a boy. Wanting a male is such a ridiculous, old-school cliché—an heir, a farmhand, a business associate to carry on the name. I knew this, but I feared having a girl child who might have weaknesses similar to my own, especially struggles with self-confidence. True, I had managed some minor successes in my life—completing graduate school with only a minimum of drug use, establishing a teaching career, and marrying a kind and intelligent man—but these outward signs of health seemed small in the face of more private facts. In high school, I had succumbed to the suburban cliché of anorexia; I had been petrified of sex for years; I had taken Prozac practically since it was invented. All these conditions had something essential in common—the tendency toward self-doubt—and I was quick to assign it a gender. When I read *Hamlet* with my high-school students, I would listen to the young prince sputter "Frailty, thy name is woman," and secretly think he should have said "self-doubt" in place of "frailty."

The irony is that I'm a big fan of the female gender. My admiration started with my mother. When I was young, I asked her about Freud—I pronounced it "Frood"—and she said, "He was a German doctor who had womb envy."

My mother was one of the early subscribers to Ms. magazine (and possibly the only one in our conservative suburb), and she volubly complained about having had to change her last name upon marriage. She had married my father at age thirty in the early 1960s, when most women were hitched by their early twenties. I listened, and took notes. During Watergate, my mother ironed while watching the hearings on TV, shaking her head at the men who had tried to ruin our country. When a famous detergent commercial came on about a woman being scolded for her husband's "ring around the collar," my mother would call out, "Tell him to wash his neck."

Despite my mother's witty social commentary, she was vulnerable to episodes of self-doubt. My mother attributes her lack of confidence to being a first-generation child of immigrants, but I did not understand this for years. As a girl, when I listened to my mother wondering if she had said the right thing to a neighbor or relative, I felt vaguely betrayed and wondered what had happened to the articulate woman who had given me an ERA Now button. Was my mother's periodic low self-esteem a punishment for her brashness in other arenas?

Five months into my pregnancy, when the ultrasound technician said, "I think I see the labia," I knew I was sentenced to dealing with the same old albatross of my gender. True, it could have worse—I might have been having twin girls—but regardless, I knew I was headed for some sort of overdue reckoning with myself. In contrast, my husband was overjoyed; he had grown up in a family of six sons and only one daughter. When we left the hospital that day, walking out into warm rain, my husband grinned and talked about names. I was more subdued, concentrating on finding awnings to duck under.

As the future mother of a daughter, I began to observe girls and young women more carefully. Teaching at a high school gave me endless opportunities. During my final trimester, two groups of students held baby showers for me, and the celebrations were radically different. The first, thrown by freshmen girls, was traditional, with pink streamers and balloons, though I had not yet revealed the gender of my baby. Several of the young women baked a pink cake for the occasion and set a small plastic doll on top of it. The doll was naked when they bought it, the girls admitted, giggling, so they had frosted a diaper on her.

The second shower, hosted by sophomore boys—their idea!—had no decorations or refreshments (I ended up ordering pizza for everyone). Activities centered on a boom box that played rap songs and other raunchy favorites, including "Get Your Freak On."

Both showers moved me, especially since my students come from financially underprivileged families and have limited resources. The boys' shower, with all its chaos, was easier for me; little was required of the guest of honor. At the girls' event, though, as soon as I saw the beribboned chair they had decorated for me, I knew that I would be on the hot seat in more ways than one. Even before I had time to taste the cake, the young women crowded in around me and demanded information: details of the pregnancy so far, possible names for the baby, even whether or not I was going to breastfeed. The young women also told me of their mothers' and sisters' pregnancies and offered advice. One girl, Melissa, went as far as to make me a list of things to pack for the hospital, including "baby mittens instead of gloves because gloves restrict their finger movement."

On the surface, the girls were confident and pro-baby, but as we talked further, more than one young woman asked me if my husband was going to be "okay" with a girl. When I told them that he actually hoped for one, they looked skeptical. One student mentioned how her mother had "finally" had a boy the year before—Galdino, Jr.—and that she often had to baby-sit for him.

I was struck by the intensity of the young women's involvement with me and my pregnancy. Looking around, I thought I even saw a certain fierceness in the pink decorations. Some of the same girls who had met to bake the cake and pooled money to buy a baby toiletry set sometimes talked back in class, swore, and passed vicious notes about each other. In a few months, Maricela, one of the shower's organizers, would be expelled from school for getting into a clawing fight in the cafeteria with her best friend, Yvette.

Sitting in my crêpe-paper throne, I felt a different sort of challenge from my fourteen-year-old students: I had to prove that I was ready to be a mother, especially if the color of the streamers proved prescient.

Giving birth frightened me. While many women I know consider the physical act of childbirth a sacred event, I was content and even relieved to agree to a cesarean. Every time I explain the term "caesura" to a class (usually while reading *Beowulf*), though, I pause when I think of the root, the Roman conqueror. My surgeon, Dr. Gupta, was a petite woman, but the method through which she delivered my daughter was named after a bellicose man.

We named Charlotte in honor of two great women: Charlotte Brontë and my mother's doctor, who was then one of the few female physicians in the suburb where I grew up. So after Charlotte was born, when people I did not know very well showered me with frilly, pink baby clothes, I believed they had missed the point. I wrote thank you notes and promptly deposited the pastel togs in donation bags. "Pink!" I exclaimed to feminist friends; but as with most matters involved in motherhood, I had more to learn. Several months later, my husband, a journalist, would interview a lesbian couple who had adopted two girls from China. Neither of the mothers was especially feminine in dress, but the girls loved everything pink and ruffled. "Before, there wasn't a stitch of pink in the house," one of the mothers told my husband. "But they love playing princess."

I like the irony and humor of this story. It also reminds me to moderate some of my responses—it stands to reason that if I outlaw pink from the household, Charlotte will crave nothing but, just as I fear that someday she will feel honor-bound to receive a D in high school English or to join the Young Republicans. (Currently, as a three-year-old, my daughter has a serious jones for all things feminine. Though she has several Latina dolls and an African American veterinarian Barbie, she is most partial to a tiny, plastic Belle from *Beauty and the Beast*. Charlotte also owns two tutus and frequently asks to wear a sundress, even in winter. On our doormat sit a pair of sparkly pink shoes from Target given to her by my mother, who at least asked my permission first about the color. When Charlotte wears them, they leave a small film of glitter in her wake.)

When I returned to teaching after my daughter's birth, my high school seniors were beginning *Frankenstein*. Even a surface reading of Mary Shelley's gothic novel reveals the author's ambivalence and confusion about motherhood. When Shelley wrote *Frankenstein* at the age of seventeen, she was unmarried, had already given birth to one premature baby who died, and was pregnant with another. The book began, famously, with a challenge to write a ghost story, and scholars have since pointed out that at the time, Shelley was tortured with dreams of her infant daughter who died. Compounding Shelley's predicament was the fact that her own mother, the groundbreaking feminist Mary Wollstonecraft Shelley, had died as a result of giving birth to her.

Teaching *Frankenstein* as a new mother was unsettling, especially since I also had pregnant students sitting in front of me—two seniors who were due to deliver before prom. One had laminated the ultrasound of her baby on her folder. When I mentioned some of the feminist readings of the novel to the class, of the "monster" as a stand-in for the burden of motherhood, I glanced anxiously at the pregnant students, but they appeared unfazed. The rest of the students, however, responded with some unease. "Having a child is the happiest moment in a mother's life," began a male student's paper about the book. The presumption reminded me of an email I had received from a former colleague after Charlotte's birth, which said, "Aren't you just about to burst with joy?"

Though violent, Mary Shelley's writing was perversely reassuring: It comforted me to read the story of a bright and confident young man having second thoughts about creating as he was pursued literally and metaphorically by his offspring.

Marta, my daughter's caregiver, believes that children are the greatest source of joy in a household, regardless of seeming obstacles. Raised in a family of eleven children in a small Mexican town, Marta was a young woman when she crossed over the border illegally to take a factory job in Chicago. Later, after she became a resident with amnesty in the 1980s, Marta married. She hoped to have many children, despite her and her husband's limited incomes, but unfortunately, she could have only two. I met Marta through her son, a former student who impressed me with his kindness, responsibility, and regard for young children.

When I went back to work three months after Charlotte's birth, I often arrived at Marta's house in the morning riddled with anxiety—about whether I had included everything in the diaper bag or satisfactorily finished my lesson plans for the day. Marta, however, would emerge from her peeling apartment building, rush to the car, and peer into the backseat at Charlotte. "My heaven, my beautiful heart," she would say in Spanish, cooing.

Marta showed me the art and passion involved in childcare. She also gloried in everything feminine: Marta urged me to have Charlotte's ears pierced and bought her small, frilly outfits. One day, when Charlotte was still an infant, Marta told me that she had been holding the baby up to the window that afternoon in the winter light. "Your daughter has amazing coloring," she said in Spanish. "I couldn't stop staring at her."

It took me longer to achieve rhapsodic moments as a mother. The first few months were an anxious stretch, a departure from my old life and strange stalling period. I found periodic moments of peace while nursing my daughter or tickling her, but I still felt like an imposter, a poorly pre- pared sham. When I hugged and kissed my daughter in public, an inner voice often asked if I was doing it just for show. I began to remember the advice of my sister- and brother-in-law: "Don't feel bad if it takes a while to fall in love with your baby."

Fortunately, Charlotte's personality began to evince itself. A simple but important moment in our relationship occurred when she was nine months old. On a walk one summer morning, I finally realized that she had her own indomitable spirit. It was late August, almost time for me to return to school. The summer had been difficult; on days when I took Charlotte to Marta's, I felt guilty and unable to work, and on days when she was with me, I berated myself for not interacting with her in a more meaningful way. Walks were one of the few ways in which we were at peace, albeit tempo- rarily. On that August morning we had just been to the coffee shop where Charlotte sipped juice and I ordered my usual strong brew.

We were heading north toward the lake when we encountered an older woman walking a Pekingese. Charlotte chortled and reached from her stroller. Though the woman paused, she appeared annoyed, like the manager of a fancy restaurant at the sight of a family with children. I was getting ready to move on with the stroller when suddenly Charlotte ripped off her small sunglasses and placed them on the dog's face. To the dog's credit, and her owner's, the Pekingese did not bolt. As Charlotte grinned and clapped, I realized with relief that my daughter had a sturdy spirit; it would take a considerable amount to dampen it.

As soon as Charlotte began to speak, in both English and Spanish, I relaxed. Some might say a child's becoming verbal is also the beginning of potential conflict (of backtalk), but I found the increased communication invigorating. Suddenly both my daughter and I were able to begin explaining ourselves; the emergence of my daughter's voice literally gave me back my own.

Not so long ago, I believed that admitting to questions or concerns about women's roles meant that I had given up on my own gender. The contradiction filled me with shame—if I felt conflict with my divergent pulls and ambitions, I wondered, how could I raise a girl to be a confident woman? I should have learned the lesson from therapy: When I told a wise psychologist I wanted to rid recurring anxieties from my mind, she objected. "I have trouble with expulsion," she said. "I'm more for recognizing what's inside."

These days, I no longer try to hide my frequent, lingering questions about gender roles and motherhood. In fact, I have decided that it will not hurt my daughter to expose her to a variety of viewpoints. Last Christmas, when my family and I sat down to watch *Beauty and the Beast*, a movie given to Charlotte by a relative, I paused the film at the beginning and temporarily blocked the screen. "First, a message from Gloria Steinem," I said. "Women, you don't have to tame monsters to make them into nice men."

My husband and brother-in-law, a psychology professor, promptly began to whistle at me and make catcalls. "Good-looking broad," they said. "Check her out." Through it all, the message and the melee, my daughter sat on the couch, observing.

Having a daughter has been both a challenge and a source of unexpected tenderness, of affection I did not always think I deserved. Recently, Charlotte announced that she wanted to marry me. When I asked her why, she said, "Remember you told me two women could get married?" I nodded, and my daughter continued: "You're the perfect woman for me."

Shining, Shimmering, Splendid

KIM FISCHER

My three-year-old triplets are playing with some friends on the small city street in front of our townhouse. They wear their dress-up clothes: sequined skirts of lace and taffeta, sparkling tiaras, necklaces of colorful beads. They hold magic wands. One of the boys on the street who is around their age is also dressed up: He is Spiderman, mask and all.

My girls skip and twirl from one side of the street to the other. Occasionally, one of my daughters hides behind a tree and coyly calls for help from one of the boys. But the boys ignore her. They run and growl and ride bikes. Spiderman charges after them with a plastic toy sword—an item from a pirate costume, I am guessing.

Watching my girls, I am amazed. I have tried to downplay the "princess thing" from the beginning. I didn't make it a big deal, I just didn't encourage my girls to look up to these princesses as ideal beauties, or to rely on stories of Prince Charming riding up on a white horse as the guiding principle for their future lives.

But despite my best efforts, one of my daughters introduces herself to people as "Jasmine" and somehow knows the lyrics to "A Whole New World" by heart. Another daughter, having reached a formal agreement with me to wear *regular* dresses and even pants and shorts to preschool, immediately changes into her Cinderella outfit as soon as she arrives home every day. And my third daughter refers to herself as "Sleeping Judy." We haven't bothered to correct her on that one. Sleeping Judy definitely makes more sense as a name anyway.

We learned we were having triplets when I was six weeks pregnant. Anthony and I were ecstatic. We assumed the babies would arrive in some combination of both genders—two girls and a boy, two boys and a girl. Twelve weeks into my pregnancy, I had the CVS test done. When the hospital called with the test results—all healthy—I was relieved. When they told me I was having three girls, I was shocked.

All girls was a combination I hadn't expected. The chances that I would, or even could, get pregnant again were slim. In that one moment I knew I would never have a boy.

But once I moved past my initial disappointment I was excited. My girls would have the sisters I always wanted but never had growing up. My girls could share secrets, share a room, and share a wardrobe. Imagine having three times the number of shoes to choose from! I even tried to calculate how long it would be before I too might be able to borrow some of their shoes. I was convinced this was going to be a blast.

But other people felt the need to remind me that the years ahead would not be one huge party. When I told my hair stylist I was expecting three girls, she said, "Oh my god, they're going to love each other and hate you!"

I tried to reassure myself that her statement was of course based solely on her own personal experiences with her particular two sisters and mother, but the truth behind it concerned me. Perhaps with two sisters, my girls would not need me very much. The fear of exclusion provoked in me by my stylist's comment was only compounded when it was coupled with the other, more common response to my announcement: "Oh, three Daddy's girls!"

However it turned out—whether we'd share some all-girl solidarity or whether they'd be "Daddy's girls" all the way—I knew I was in for the mother–daughter experience . . . times three.

I have two hopes for my girls: I want them each to have their own unique personalities; and I want them each to have a strong sense of identity as girls and women. In some ways, those are the same hope—emerging, I suppose, from my own years spent experimenting with three-toned eye shadow, testing too-tight perms, plucking my eyebrows way too thin, dabbling in diets and eating disorders. My own years figuring out what it means to be a girl.

So far, so good. Even though my girls all love to dress up as identical princesses, they definitely have three distinct personalities—something that was apparent virtually from birth. In the hospital, it was Cinderella who was often awake and frequently crying, as if she had something important to communicate; Jasmine was the one most at ease and comfortable, happy to hang out with the intensive-care nurses until she could go home; and, weighing a little less at birth than her sisters, Sleeping Judy had the most determination, overcoming minor medical problems and catching up to her siblings. Their personalities today are consistent with their behavior in those first few weeks. Cinderella is the "big sister," watching out for the others and negotiating conflicts; Jasmine is extremely confident in social situations, a natural leader; and Sleeping Judy is the most physically ambitious of the three, always willing to leap from any height.

With numerous gifts from generous family and friends, it would have been impossible to declare our home a Princess-Free Zone. So I allow the pink and the jewelry and the fairy tales, but at the same time I make a conscious effort to model my own example of what is possible for girls. I'm proud, for example, when I see Cinderella and Jasmine pair off now and then and pretend to be "Mommy and Margot"—my 6:00 AM jogging partner—"running a marathon." One day when my girls were just babies I sat on the beach at dusk with them, my sister-in-law, and her two girls, watching as my husband and his brother rode the waves on an ocean kayak. When my seven-year-old niece asked me to try it, I looked at the row of us girls spectating on the sidelines and realized I had to swallow my fear and go for it. My girls were too young at the time to remember my successful glide to the shore, but I hope efforts like that one will someday provide a big return.

And the princess attire has not seemed to turn the girls into docile ladies-in-waiting. My husband sees them as characters right out of that prototypical "guy" movie, The Godfather. He casts Cinderella as Tom Hagan, the consiglieri (advisor/mediator to the group); Jasmine as Michael Corleone (umm, enough said); and Sleeping Judy as Luca Brasi (the muscle). Every time that "Tom Hagan" adopts a knowing expression and tells "Michael Corleone" to let "Luca Brasi" wear the pink tutu this time; every time that "Luca Brasi," in black patent leather Mary Janes and faux fur, chases down a kid on the street to snatch back "Michael Corleone's" toy stroller, we laugh hysterically at our pigtailed mafia.

Today as I watch my little princesses dance along the pavement, I'm a bit stymied. It's clear that society has certain expectations of girls and women. But it seems equally clear that my girls have some sort of innate instinct to identify themselves with the most stereotypical expression of girlness that there is.

With their "dress-ups," as they call them, my girls are trying on what they think it means to be a girl. I hope for more for them. I want to teach them to question traditional gender roles. I have dreams of instilling in them a sense of inner strength and independence—which are not the first things that come to mind when I think of princesses. But I realize as I watch them play that perhaps my three-year-old girls may have more to teach me about challenging assumptions than I have to teach them.

Suddenly, Spiderman lunges at Jasmine. Pointing his sword at her, he yells menacingly, "I'm going to cut you!"

Jasmine stands still, and I don't know what is going to happen. She tilts her head down and looks at him over her small, wire-framed bifocals. Then she taps Spiderman on the shoulder with her magic wand and says, "I turn you into a mountain."

Spiderman cries and runs away, shouting, "I don't want to be a mountain!"

Maybe I have been underestimating the power of princesses after all.

Ladylike

GABRIELLE SMITH-DLUHA

I'm out in my green, leafy backyard pulling weeds around sunflowers while my five-year-old daughter, Olivia, plays alongside me, collecting roly-polies in a jar and singing to herself.

I love listening to her sing while I work, laughing at her silly lyrics. But this time, I almost drop my trowel in shock when I hear her sweet little voice chant:

I don't know what
you've heard about me
I'm a motherfucking
P-I-M-P
And you won't get
A buck out of me.

"Olivia!" I gasp, hoping my neighbors on the other side of the fence haven't heard this little ditty. "Where on earth did you get that song?"

But do I really need to ask? I know. It's her two older brothers, ages thirteen and ten.

Two boys and then a girl: This had always been my dream family. And I got it. I had long cherished an image of protective male figures doting on their sweet little sister. Obviously, I never had a brother of my own. Otherwise, I would have known that having real brothers means burp-on-command lessons, a limitless repertoire of fart jokes, wrestling matches anywhere and everywhere, and an early introduction to profanity.

It's not that they don't care for their sister, and even each other, in an astoundingly tender way. They do. But brotherhood is a whole package, one with rough and ready edges. And that translates into a little sister whose preferred outfit is a pair of boxers and no shirt. A girl who *can* throw. And a daughter who packs a pretty good punch.

Ever since Olivia was born, a sister to two brothers, I've struggled with the question of what it means to be a girl. I wonder if this heavy dose of boy input is healthy for my daughter and if I'm doing enough to nurture femininity in our family. I first clued in that Olivia's identity was being strongly shaped by her brothers when I overheard her as a toddler threatening a friend that she would "punch his face in" if he didn't give back a toy truck. This has since evolved into an attraction to bad words, a strong interest in video games, and even shoving little boys down at the school carnival.

I've begun to worry: Will she grow up to be too rough and aggressive? Should I be teaching her to be more ladylike? *Ladylike?!?!* Could I actually be *thinking* the word, let alone wondering how to impart its qualities to my daughter? I'm certainly no lady. After thirteen years of raising sons, femininity has become a concept so distant and elusive, I don't know if I can find it again for Olivia's sake. If I ever even had it to begin with.

I wonder if I should be more actively encouraging Olivia's girlish side. Should I be telling her, "Olivia, quit wrestling, honey. It's time to paint your nails"? It's true, I breathe a secret sigh of relief when I see Olivia paint a rainbow with a little row of flowers underneath, or when she expresses interest in tea parties, unicorns, and beauty products. But a part of me thinks, who needs that stuff anyway? So what that she can spit with speed and accuracy, and does so frequently—isn't she still a girl?

Because of our neighborhood and the composition of her preschool class, Olivia doesn't get much playtime with other girls. It's just her brothers, Jacob and Theo; lots of their friends; her Dad—and then one lone female, me. Even our pet gerbil is a boy. It's this onslaught of male influence that I find myself struggling to resist on her behalf, even while Olivia works her heart out to stay in league with her brothers.

In the morning, Olivia rounds the corner of the stairs in Theo's over-size shorts and baggy T-shirt. Dresses and skirts? No way. She only wants to wear their hand-me-down clothes, with her blonde hair hanging long and unbrushed. Jacob has loaned her his iPod again. She's got his headphones on, and she's listening to gangsta rap. "Mom, can women rap too?" she asks me. "I want to be a rapper when I grow up."

When I ask the boys to watch Olivia, which I do a lot—when I'm cooking dinner, need to run to the store, want a minute to write, or have a good friend on the phone—they aren't the least interested in getting down on the floor with her and playing relationship games with her set of teeny porcelain fairies. No, it's football camp time in the living room, complete with push-ups, scrimmages, and touchdowns full force into the couch.

When the boys' friends are over, Olivia's up in the computer room with the pack of them clustered around a computer screen, watching as they enthusiastically construct a goblin army fortress in some middle-earth war game. When I call her to come down, she protests, "But Mom! It's my favorite game!"

It's their friends that she really wants to impress, lanky boys with fresh, eager faces, sitting around our table eating bagels after school. She's discovered that rude words seem to do the trick. Nothing gets a thirteen-year-old boy's attention and laughter quicker than the F-word from her mouth. Without such tactics, she's left out: The boys are not interested in unicorns or tea parties.

What gets me the most is not that she wants to bond with these boys, or that she's a tomboy who doesn't want to fix her hair with bows and ribbons. That's fine with me. It's that she seems to see little value in being a girl. She's often told me that she doesn't want to grow up to be a woman. Women have to cook all the time, she says. Women have to have babies. She wishes that she could grow up to be a man. Despite the fact that I have a meaningful career and that Olivia's father is an active, equal participant in our home, Olivia has somehow gotten it into her mind that being a woman is not where it's at.

When we play fantasy games, she always wants to be the leading male. She's Peter Pan and I'm Wendy. Or she's the male wolf (her brother's favorite animal) bringing home freshly hunted meat to the mother wolf (me) lying in the den and nursing the litter (a ragged assortment of stuffed elephants, bunnies, and teddy bears standing in as wolf pups). Another favorite game is to be a lead Alaskan sled dog (male) with me as an admiring female dog deeply in love with "him," despite his cool rejections time and time again.

I often try to coax her into being the mother wolf, or Wendy, or the lovesick Alaskan dog, thinking that she has to, at least *sometimes,* identify with something other than her brothers' robust masculine energy. But she insists on being the male. In response, I end up trying to affirm my feminine identity in front of her as often as I can. "I love being a woman," I'll say. Or, "I'm so glad that my body can have babies and nurse!" Or "Daddy and I are so happy that we finally had a girl!"

It's even gone so far that when she admires and envies certain prominent male body parts, I find myself saying, "Well, I love my vagina," trying to toss off that phrase as comfortably and casually as I can.

Am I sending Olivia the message that I only like her when she's a girl, when she draws pink hearts or dresses up like a princess? Or does she also know how proud I am of her when she holds her own against the boys, pinning them down in a wrestling match? Is what I see in Olivia really about Olivia at all, or merely a reflection of the issues I wrestle with as a woman myself?

In the back of my mind, I've always been haunted by an image of the ideal woman. She's always kind. She cooks and sews. She's gentle, wise, and self-sacrificing. She tenderly nurses the sick. She's a natural craftsperson and expertly jars jams and fruits. She's sexy and pretty with slim legs and delicate ankles. She's always laughing and forgiving—always.

I'm not like that, and I never have been. Sure, I can be kind and self-sacrificing when necessary. But I can also be selfish. I'm pretty and sexy in my own way, but I definitely have thunder thighs, and I don't love cooking day in and day out. I'm not that tender when people get sick—after a day or two, it's more like, "Okay, time to get over it." And I'm not crafty; I like to paint and draw, but I couldn't make a mosaic birdhouse if my life depended on it. I am not that ideal woman. And when I see Olivia in her tomboy outfit shouting out "Hike!" in our living room football camp, I know she isn't, either.

Neither are my boys, as boyish as I've described them here, stereotypical males. They have their moments of the kind of "feminine" experience I've ascribed to this ladylike überfemale I picture: helping to take care when someone gets sick, being intuitive about others, even sometimes playing with dolls.

So maybe it's the image that's a lie, and myself and Olivia who are real. Perhaps that ladylike ideal is something we can define as we go along.

When I finish up weeding around the sunflowers, I tell Olivia that her rap is good, but I'd rather she leave out the cuss words.

"Can I say 'bleep' where the bad words are?" She asks me, her eyes a pure, uncorrupted green.

I think of the lyrics from one of Jacob's new favorite songs: *Ladies is pimps too. / Kick back / and turn up your shoulders.*

I'm not exactly sure what "Ladies is pimps too" really means, or how exactly one might turn up her shoulders, but I do know how to kick back. So I tell her, "Oh, sure, all right."

I take Olivia's hand and we go for our usual late afternoon walk around the neighborhood picking blackberries. Then we wait, hidden, behind some bushes to ambush Jacob and Theo with some pinecones as they come riding up on their bikes.

"Pinecone War!" Olivia and I shout with delight as we catch the boys off-guard.

Tough Girls

REBECCA
STEINITZ

There were two options—the pink frame decorated with pink and purple flowers or the black and blue frame decorated with green paw prints—but there was no choice. It was time to buy my oldest daughter her first bicycle, and I was not, I repeat, not going to get her a girly bike. Luckily the bike clearly meant for boys could easily be framed as neutral, especially to a four-year-old girl who just wanted off her tricycle.

We all loved the "Blue's Clues" bike, as we immediately dubbed it, even though the paw prints were green. With training wheels, Mara whizzed down the neighborhood sidewalks that first summer, and the next year she learned to ride on two wheels in a single afternoon on the basketball court. But by the end of that summer, when I saw how frantically she pedaled to keep up with her friends and how, with her feet on the pedals, her knees almost reached her ears, I knew we had to move on.

This time it wasn't so easy. I immediately turned away from the requisite girl's bike, but the alternative—red and black with racing stripes and a thick bar—screamed boy! I yearned for a green paw print, but we had entered the realm of big-kid bikes, and that was no longer an option. The new bicycle was going to be a Hanukkah present, so Mara wasn't even with us when we chose, but I just couldn't do it. This was a girl who wore a dress every day from the age of eighteen months, who loved ballet and fashion, whose favorite color was indisputably pink, who would be thrilled beyond her wildest dreams by a pink bike with a flowered seat, white basket, and streamers on the handlebars. When it came down to her desires and my principles, there was no contest.

I'm your basic old-style feminist. I subscribed to Ms. magazine as a teenager, I count the women on the podium and in the table of contents, I walk out of movies with gratuitous violence against women, and I always believe the woman when it comes down to he said/she said. When I got pregnant, I painted the crib lilac-blue and bought yellow and green baby clothes. When I gave birth to girls, I proudly accepted hand-me-down gray and blue sweatpants from the little boys we knew, and I filled the toy shelves with trucks, paints, and blocks. When I realized that all the board books were about boy bunnies, I sent my feminist mother off to the feminist bookstore, where she got us our very own copy of Hard Hatted Women's Painting Our Way to a Better Future: An Art/Coloring Book of Contemporary Options for Women (that's really the title), which is all about grandmothers who lay pipes and aunts who climb telephone poles. And we read it every night, too.

But contemporary American girldom is hard to resist, especially when you have a girl with no interest in resisting. First it was the dresses. I really didn't care what she wore, so long as she was warm enough in winter and dry enough in rain, and red, blue, and purple jersey dresses over equally colorful leggings make a pretty good look for a three-year-old. Besides, I wear dresses and skirts to work almost every day, so how could I refuse? Then came pink. I tried to steer her to the boy's racks at the used clothing stores, holding up lovely red plaid shirts and blue and green striped sweaters, but she would have none of it, heading straight for the pink—the more sequined and sparkly, the better. The trucks and trains went unplayed with, except when boys came over, and dress-ups and dolls were the indisputable favorites.

So far it's a familiar story. The feminist mom confronts the limits of her ability to shape her daughter's gender predilections. At this point, the feminist mom usually arrives at one of two conclusions. Either she announces that she has been converted to the power of biology and realizes that boys really are boys and girls really are girls and there's nothing she can do about it, or she condemns the effectiveness of the cultural machinery that puts baby girls in pink blankets as soon as they are born and allows no alternatives to the boy and girl aisles at Toys R Us—except puzzles, and who really wants to play with puzzles anyway?

However, watching Mara on her pink bike, I realized that it wasn't as simple as either nature or nurture. Mara was a kick-ass bike rider. Learning to ride without training wheels in a single day was only the beginning. A few weeks later, we went out on the bike path, and she rode six miles with hardly a break. As we rode around town one day, she wiped out going down a hill—the kind of wipeout that brings people sitting on their porches out to the street with wet washcloths and bandages. But after a few tears and a sparkly Band-Aid, she got right back up on that pink bike and kept going. Would it have made a difference if her bike had been red or blue or orange? I don't think so.

Actually, Mara and her younger sister, Eva, usually don't cry when they fall down. They don't look to adults for help or lie prostrate on the ground. They just get up—unless they're really hurt. Long ago, a friend pointed out to me that when a girl falls down we rush to her, asking if she is okay and picking her up to comfort her before she even realizes she needs comfort, but when a boy falls down, we just let him get up. I realized she was right. So when I had daughters of my own and they started to walk and thus, inevitably, to fall, I didn't respond. I didn't ask if they were okay; I didn't rush to their sides; I just waited to see what happened. If they were hurt, they cried—and then, of course, I rushed to them, picked them up, and comforted them. But if they weren't hurt, they looked around, realized they were fine, and got up. As a result, Mara and Eva are tough, and they never fake it: They know that if they need us we'll be there, but they also know that most of the time they can handle things on their own.

In fact, my girls are hard-core minifeminists. Eva likes nothing better than climbing a climbing wall. Furious that there have been no women presidents, Mara is ready to run for office as soon as she's old enough. Eva thinks daddies cook better than mommies (and in our house, she's right). Mara writes letters to the principal of her school about how unfair it is that the boys get three-fourths of the playground just because they like to play soccer and football. They worship Venus and Serena and Natalie Coughlin, the Olympic backstroke champion. They think it's okay for families to have two mommies or two daddies—or just one mommy or one daddy. They know they can do whatever they want when they grow up, and they know we need to keep working to eliminate poverty and discrimination so that all kids can do whatever they want when they grow up.

How did I do it? Unabashed brainwashing. I tell them they are strong and capable and can be anything they want to be. I show them powerful women. Whenever they talk about what boys do, I remind them that girls can do it too, and vice versa. I point out injustices, and together we try to do something about them. Now they do it on their own—after we went to our first lesbian wedding in Massachusetts last summer, Mara came home and wrote to the governor of Ohio, asking him to make gay marriage legal so that children could be happy and people could do what they want.

But I also let them do what they want. I realized pretty quickly that it wasn't fair to try to keep them in sweatpants as they watched me put on lipstick and high heels before a party. How could I refuse them their dolls when I loved my *Vogue*? And if I could wear lipstick and high heels, read *Vogue,* and still understand and take action against systemic gender discrimination, couldn't I let them wear pink dresses and play with dolls and still teach them that girls and boys are equal?

In some ways, it all comes down to Barbie (doesn't it always?). When I was a kid, I had a Barbie. I washed her hair with shampoo and then cut it all off when it turned to straw. I magic-markered red rouge onto her cheeks and blue shadow onto her eyelids. I may even have made her a few outfits. And I'm a still feminist, because along with the Barbie, there was a *Ms.* magazine on the coffee table, and there were books about women and women's rights on the bookshelves, and my mom and my dad both worked and both took care of us, and they told me I could be whatever I wanted to be.

At last count, Mara and Eva have eight Barbies. I don't buy them— they were all birthday presents from friends, mostly boys—but I don't make a fuss over them. Sometimes the girls play with them, most often when they receive a new one, but mainly they just live in a box that we decorated with fashion pictures cut out from magazines. I won't buy them Barbie clothes or backpacks, but they do have a Barbie skateboard—also a gift, only it doesn't work very well, so it generally gets ignored in favor of the scooter, inline skates, and pink bikes. But why should I worry about Barbie when they also have books about women politicians and construction workers? When they go to rallies for women's rights? When they have a mother and father who both go to work and take care of them and tell them they can wear whatever they want to wear, so long as it's warm in winter and dry in rain, and be whatever they want to be, so long as they keep helping us change the world?

A few weeks ago I took Eva to buy new sneakers. Unlike Mara, who started emphatically stating her preferences before she was two, Eva, at three, is just discovering her own desires. She wants baby dolls, and at the shoe store she wanted the sneakers with pink flowers. I had my usual pang of frustration, but I bought them, because part of bringing up a feminist girl is letting her make her own choices. The next day I watched her climb to the top of the climbing wall without stopping: my tough girl in pink sneakers.

Confessions of a Tomboy Mom

JACQUELYN MITCHARD

The doctor was late.

She'd been at a Christmas party and came rushing into the room only seconds before my firstborn daughter slipped into my open hands from the body of her birthmother.

Why was I adopting a child? It was an eccentric choice. I had three sons already. Nearing forty, I'd been widowed the previous year. The idea of adding a new family member had prompted more than a few raised eyebrows (not to mention raised voices) in my extended family. Nevertheless, here we were, two single moms—one possibly too old and one certainly too young—bringing into the world a new baby, while in the hall at this Methodist hospital, a choir of nurses sang about yet a third single mother and her baby in the manger.

And then, there she was, big and bonny, too curious about the world to cry. A beautiful little—*girl?* A moment of panic sliced through my joy: What in the name of all that was sensible was I going to do with a girl?

I'd never played with dolls. I'd been sent home from first grade (in the '60s) for being the only girl to wear capri pants to the first day of school instead of the required skirt. My greatest joy, back then, was attaching long pieces of Scotch tape to my toes, a la *National Velvet*, and pretending to ride great horses. I did this until I was a young teen, when I had saved enough summer and birthday money to buy my own horse. I think the only times that I wore a dress before my wedding were for my senior prom and a job interview.

Since becoming the sole provider for a family of four, I supposed I'd grown to identify more with the guy side of my personality. No one opened the door for me; in fact, my sons thought it was funny to lock me out. And if I didn't rake those leaves in the yard, they stayed there until spring.

Still, somehow, I'd pictured myself doing with my own little girl all the things my friends relished doing with theirs—shopping and preening, dressing up and confiding, playing with a dollhouse (which would be my first, as well as hers), and, as she grew up, understanding everything mothers and daughters share.

But there in the delivery room, I panicked. I didn't know about any of that stuff! I had acute mall-o-phobia! I wasn't any more interested in dolls now than I'd been when I was four! I still wanted to jump on the trampoline with my sons, play boxing, pillow-fight, and water ski! All the clothes I'd saved for the fourth child were embossed with trucks and soccer balls!

I'd never had a moment's doubt about raising my boys. Somehow, I understood them; and their needs were . . . well, rather simple. They liked lots of good food, lots of rough-and-tumble fun, lots of hugs, lots of sand, lots of objects of various sizes to use as props in our favorite parlor game:

If This Balloon/Ball/Frisbee Hits the Ground, The World Blows Up. Now, they weren't NASCAR boys—while they played sports, they also played piano. They endured the mandatory reading of *Little Women* and *Charlotte's Web* I considered essential to human development, and, to my joy, they ended up loving those books. Each of them had rag dolls and teddy bears (my eldest son just got his own apartment, and among the things he packed were Puffy and Tony). And their father, as well as I, never failed to kiss them goodnight—something I continue to do, even into their teens. Simply put, I thought of boys as children—the basic model. I had the operating manual. I knew how to do it.

What if I did all that with the little girl I'd named Francie? Would she turn out, against her nature, to be a lumberjack girl? Would I be cheating her, and myself, of the intimate joys of Barbies, bunnies, and bows?

I couldn't take the chance. Having mastered, to some degree, being a woman, I set about learning how to be a girl.

I bought wallpaper with flowers. I bought fuzzy toys with big, wide-set eyes. For her baptism, I befrilled my Francie in every piece of eyelet in the marketplace—a bonnet as big as a sunflower and booties with pink ribbons interwoven among the creamy yarn. For her first birthday, her denim one-piece jumper also was bedecked in lace and featured a tam. (I had to glue it to a piece of her hair to keep her from tugging it off—a trick I learned from a neighbor; to this day, I am ashamed.)

Meanwhile, Francie's three older brothers learned to adore her. Though she didn't fill the great hole in our hearts left by their father's early death from cancer, she brought breath back into our house. They learned to change her diapers, helped her to enjoy being thrown back and forth between them, and rolled her in sand like a tortilla in brown sugar. She learned to walk at nine months and to climb (onto the counter, up the tree fort ladder, up the stairs) long before that. When a relative gave her a Barbie doll (well, it *was* a Dentist Barbie), the boys banned it to the donation box before she could catch sight of it. "Do you want her to be a sissy girl," my middle son, Dan, demanded, "and grow up to be one of those girls who pretend they aren't smart?"

Well, heck, no.

One morning, when I'd dressed her lovingly for church in a white dress with red-apple buttons, I was interrupted by a phone call. When I turned around, I suddenly saw Francie, then thirteen months old, standing at the top of a short staircase, methodically pulling those little apples off, one by one, and dropping them down the heat vent. As I gestured wildly to one of the boys to stop her, she whipped off her dress and returned in her chosen church clothes—a gray Toledo Mud Hens T-shirt that hung slightly below her chubby knees and above the tops of her Elefanten shoes.

Fast-forward eight years.

On her report card, Francie's teacher, who absolutely adores her, writes, "It's certainly easy to tell that Francie is the younger sister of three older brothers!" After a semester of dance, she joined the swim club and is now developing the shoulders of a little athlete. Being a girl is no impediment, but no big deal either. It has cost her some fellowship on the playground, where she'd rather swing and climb while the other girls play with and trade tiny Disney or Hello Kitty figures. But she doesn't seem to mind. Her two best pals are Kellen and Conor—they call themselves "the three amigos"—and she still throws overhand. On Mondays, I get to pick the school outfits for her and also for her little sister (did I mention Mimi, who came along just nine months to the day after I remarried, when Francie was two?). I always choose the one skirt and one pretty sweater each of them owns, or a pair of pants without raggedy bottoms and holes, and they put up with my *oohs* and *aahs* after a ritual protest. But why should they be otherwise? I'm up and into some variation of exercise clothes or dungarees every morning, and so is their father. When I come downstairs in a skirt, they ask me where I'm giving a speech.

Of course, little Mimi was going to be my "girly girl," a dainty darling from day one, and for years, she did fancy crinolines wider than she was tall and fetching skirts and tops from Oilily (via eBay). Then, this year, entering kindergarten, Mimi decided she was going to stick to blue jeans and striped T-shirts "just like Sissy," and since I'm getting a little long in the tooth for the possibility of *another* daughter, I think my destiny is to raise outdoorsy instead of clotheshorsey people.

Sometimes I look at other mothers and daughters, in matching outfits, with little purses and Mary Jane shoes, and sigh. Other times, I take comfort in knowing that multiple research studies have shown that tomboy girls grow up to be both attractive to men (if not boys) and successful in the work they choose to do. So, oh well. My girls don't play "bride" or "rock star." I'm not that keen on how female rock stars behave and dress, and I'm in no rush to see either of them walking down the aisle to become grownups. They play "Phantom of the Cow Opera" with their elaborate farm play set and their Groovy Girl dolls, whose faces have faded from numerous "diving lessons" in the tub. Their chosen décor involves seals and seashells instead of puppies and princesses.

I guess they are their mother's daughters, for better or worse.

Still, there was a moment the other day that was both poignant and revealing. I'd taken Francie for a haircut. Francie's hair is magnificent—it's truly black, and you can bury your fingers in its thickness as you might into the pelt of a Newfoundland dog. It hangs to her elbows like a straight sheet of silk, with a tiny wave just at the ends. But after years of fighting the battle of the brush and ponytail band, and with swimming much on her mind, she'd decided to cut it short, up to the ears, and I was all for it—outside my bedroom door. Inside, I was crying into my pillow, realizing just how much that sweet black river of hair certified me as the mother of a girl.

With the hairstylist's cape around her shoulders, Francie's great brown eyes suddenly misted over.

"Mama," she asked, "Do I have to get my hair cut off?"

"Why, you wanted your hair cut off!" I gasped, "You said it would be so easy, and you'd never have to brush out the tangles. . . ."

"I know. But now, really I don't," Francie said, "It's pretty. And grown-ups always tell me they want it. And I like the attention . . . and I don't know why . . . but . . . I guess, for now, I'd rather keep it. Is that okay?"

"Francie, of course," I told her, sending up prayers of secret thanksgiving.

"After all," she said softly, "I *am* a girl."

Girl House

YVONNE
LATTY

'm gay and I got pregnant via artificial insemination.

All the articles I read said that if you have a baby this way you are more likely to have a boy. I had a pointy, high stomach, which, I was told by various experienced mothers, meant I was having a boy. The Chinese horoscope on the Internet predicted I was having a boy. My partner and I had a contest for our friends and family to guess the baby's birth date, weight, and sex; of the twenty-five people who participated, only two guessed that I would have a girl. But the absolute fail-proof reason why I was sure to have a boy was offered by my Latino mother and her friends. They had me wait in the kitchen while they hid a pair of scissors and a knife under two fancy embroidered pillows. I was then told to pick the pillow that felt the most "attractive" to me. I chose the pillow with a knife underneath it, which meant I was having a boy. That test is never wrong, the women told me as they congratulated me on the impending birth of my son. The only diversion from the boy predictions all around us was a good family friend who said she didn't care if we were having a boy or a girl: She just wanted to know if we were having a lesbian.

So it seemed fated that we would have a boy. My partner and I tried to encourage each other. We told each other that it would be great raising little Isaac. It would be fun. It would be different, for sure, but we would be good at it. We read up on circumcision and felt ready to deal with the penis. I love sports, he'd have caring uncles as father figures, and we would do everything we could to make him happy. It was all going to be good.

But I'd never had a brother, let alone a son, and all my close relationships were with women. I was scared of the unknown. Deep down inside, I was nervous.

After twenty-one hours of natural childbirth, in which I cried and screamed through what felt like near-death pain, I pushed out a healthy 7.8-pound baby. It was quickly placed on my stomach. I looked at it, with its dark almond-shaped eyes, full red lips, and head full of straight, jet-black hair, but I was in a fog. I didn't know what to make of it. I heard my partner ask, "What is it?" And I said, "It's a boy."

My midwife plucked the baby out of my arms, checked its private parts, and announced, "It's a girl."

My partner began crying, I'm not sure if they were tears of joy or relief, but I was in shock. "A girl?"

"What's her name?" my midwife asked.

We were so sure we were having a boy, we had barely considered a girl's name. I almost said "Isaac," but I caught myself.

"Nola," I said.

That was the beginning of life with Nola.

Nola isn't just any little girl. She is a pink-loving, curly-haired, princess-adoring, I-must-wear-a-dress-every-day, paint-my-nails-and-toenails-please, I-am-so-beautiful kind of girl. Nola is a graceful ballerina who loves her dolls and stuffed animals. She hates wearing jeans and prefers shoes to sneakers. She is about as feminine as feminine can be, and she's got two moms, who, though not hard-core butch types, have never been known to wear long, flowing dresses to go to the playground—much to her dismay.

As a kid, I was tomboy. I loved sports, roughhousing, and trading baseball cards. I hated wearing dresses and never had a princess phase or anything remotely like it. I felt more comfortable with a basketball in my hand than a purse. But mothering my little girl has given me a second chance at girlhood. I've rented countless princess videos, watching them over and over and again with her, even acting out scenes together. I have to admit I'm disappointed that she never lets me play the princess—instead I'm the evil stepmother, fairy godmother, and the prince. We play dress-up, baby dolls, and Barbie. The neighbors have heard me cheering my lungs out when we play cheerleader, and I enjoy holding up my end of the conversation as a lady at an elegant tea party. I can often be found prancing around the kitchen with Nola, the Nutcracker ballet blasting on the CD player, doing my best imitation of a graceful ballerina.

In Nola's six-year-old world there is no limit to what a woman can be and do. She was thrilled by the Disney World "princess breakfast," as princess after princess joined our table for a photo, but I saw the same thrill on her face when I watched her slowly and proudly change a light bulb for the first time. She'll ask how plumbing works while being decked out in a fancy dress-up costume. Nola helped me pick out the perfect bra at Victoria's Secret, and she comments on all my lipstick choices, but she gets an equal charge from coming with me to book signings, always offering to help me carry and set up my books. She surprised me the other day when she started kicking a soccer ball around her aunt's backyard with real accuracy and grace. I was ready to sign her up for soccer, but I caught myself: What I was watching was the influence of ballet on sports, not a girl who purely loves sports the way I did. Nola is her own woman.

Recently my partner and I celebrated twelve years together, and we had a big party. Nola was there, dressed in the white flower-girl dress she wore just weeks before at her cousin's wedding. She wants to wear that poofy white dress every day.

Back home, spending the night with her grandmother, was her little sister, Margo, who was supposed to be Edward or David according to the Chinese Horoscope; the knife under the pillow; my pointy, high stomach; and the sex, birth date, and weight contest.

Go figure.

Cheerleader

MIRIAM
PESKOWITZ

My daughter likes girls and all things girly—the girlier and tartier the better. She adores Hillary Duff, even though it's a rare vacation day that she's allowed to watch *Lizzie McGuire* on TV. *The Princess Diaries 2* CD is standard fare during our first-grade-bound morning drive time, and I can no longer count how many times she's seen the video. She likes her shorts rolled up as short as shorts can be, with the waistband tucked over, the way the thirteen-year-olds wear it. She loves summer, when she can wear a skimpy bathing suit all day long: I have many an end-of-summer bus photo of Samira, hopping off wearing nothing more than a tankini with the top pulled high, duffle bag slung over her shoulder.

My daughter also, and especially, likes cheerleading—or at least the accessories of cheerleading. On a trip with her grandma to visit the American Girl Place in Manhattan, Samira browsed in search of the perfect something to fit her $20 budget. Out of an entire store of bright outfits, shiny books about cool things to do with your hair and the adventures of sixteenth-century Native American girls, and videos of bright-eyed innocents who save their best friends from an orphanage life of hard factory labor, my daughter was drawn to the yellow and blue sheen of the miniature pompoms accompanying the American Girl cheerleading outfit.

If you ask her, she'll tell you the best birthday party she ever attended was Jeannette's. Jeannette's mom and dad gave everyone shiny purple pompoms. Jeannette's older cousin Sarah—a real live high-school cheerleader—taught the six-year-olds key cheerleading moves and chants. She belted out the cheers for all of Philadelphia's major sports teams. She gave the girls pompom instructions. She even demonstrated the kind of splits where you begin standing and you end with one leg bent in front and the other bent behind, arms held high, up, and out in a triumphal V—and, of course, with a perfect full smile on your face. My daughter loved that party. She bounced home that afternoon, shiny purple pompoms in tow, elated to tell me all about it. I watched as she showed off her new skills. I tried not to be the dour, downer mom.

A week or so after that cheerleading party, Samira's friend Megan came home with us after school. The two girls scrounged around the dress-up trunk and emerged with—what else—cheering outfits. Samira strutted about in a spaghetti-strap number paired with a bright blue shiny skating skirt, short and tarty. Megan squeezed herself into an old pink-spotted jaguar outfit that someone had given Samira for a much earlier birthday. They jolted into the bedroom, where I was folding laundry, wanting to show me their outfits and their cheers.

"And mom, you know, cheering teaches us to spell," Samira pointed out. "That makes it good! We can spell 'Philadelphia'—no f's."

I was not in a sporting mood. I launched into a mom version of the History Channel, telling them that cheerleading reminded me of times when girls weren't allowed to play organized sports, when we couldn't be at the center of attention except as smiling beauties.

My daughter and her friend are both daughters of feminist moms, and both daughters of writers. They're used to their mothers passing down mysterious, impassioned fragments about the once-upon-a-time tormented life of girls—and then telling them why they can't do really fun stuff, like cheerlead, or hang out at the mall (not a real possibility for them at six and seven, but something they learned from Polly Pockets), or buy all the really cool high-fashion clothes for girls they see at the stores (trendy teenwear shrunk to fit elementary-school bodies). I imagine they're used to hearing these strange ramblings from us every so often. Which isn't to say they can make sense of it.

Is my generation of now-forty-something women the last to remember some of these struggles played out in our own 1970s elementary school days? Even as I write, it sounds so far away. I was born in 1964. One of my kindergarten memories is learning to write the date—1969—on the proper line on the worksheet, next to my name. I left elementary school in 1976, the bicentennial year, when we all learned to play fifes and role-play colonial times for the end-of-year pageant. If ideals of equity between boys and girls weren't yet the norm in my neighborhood, they were on their way to becoming our nation's statute law.

In 1975, President Gerald Ford signed the final regulations of Title IX of the Education Amendments of 1972. The preamble read: "*No person in the United States shall, on the basis of sex, be excluded from participation in, be denied the benefits of, or be subject to discrimination under any educational programs or activity receiving federal financial assistance.*" The new laws affected schools, colleges and universities, museums, libraries, and all other institutions that received federal funds. These laws opened up to women all the schools and universities and programs that had before limited their enrollment to men. They also changed school sports: No longer could girls' athletics be ignored. But it took some time for things to change.

To comply with Title IX, for one week, our gym teachers opened the doors between the girls' and boys' gyms—for this was more than thirty years ago, when girls and boys had gym class in separate rooms—and announced we'd be square dancing. The boys lined up on one side, the girls on the other. The boys were told to walk across the large expanse between us and pick a girl partner. This was supposed to satisfy the Title IX requirement of equal physical education for girls and boys. After that week, the boys returned to learning baseball and basketball skills. We girls went back to dance routines and tumbling, acts I now understand as pre-cheerleading skills, gym for girls.

Years later, in 1999, my daughter is nearly a year old. It's July and hot, and we wander into an Italian café so I can get a cold drink. The overhead TV is on, and it's the finals of the Women's World Cup. The U.S. team is playing China, the score is tied, and five soccer players have lined up for overtime penalty kicks. It's tense in the café as everyone watches. Kick after kick, the Americans make their goals; so do the Chinese, except for one, and then we face the final moment, when Brandi Chastain, last in the line-up, zips that American ball past the Chinese goalkeeper's arms. The stands roar as the American soccer players win, and that's when Brandi famously rips off her soccer shirt in triumph and swings it overhead, pumping her hands in the air, now wearing only her black sports bra, long soccer shorts, shin guards, and cleats.

I'm in tears. I can't help it. Watching women win, watching women take center stage and work hard and sweat and be thrilled and filled with wonder when they succeed, lifting their arms overhead—not with a forced, pretty smile, but with proud, accomplished eyes—that does it for me. Samira's watching too, from below. She's smiling because everyone in the café is shouting and happy. She has no idea why we cheer. But it's that feeling I want for my daughter, and I want it to come more easily and in more situations than it did for girls of my generation. That's my worry about the cheerleading and all the girly stuff: It distracts the next generation of daughters. We think everything's okay, when it's not; when after all's said and done, we couldn't even sustain a professional women's soccer league, even though our soccer-playing women played well and won.

I love my daughter's attention to girls and friendship, and to her own happy body and the different outfits she can try out. I think it's great that she alternates girly clothes with the oversized sweatshirts and jeans and boots she wears all winter long. I love that she walks easily in the world. It's just the world out there: Do I trust it?

During one of our family discussions about cheerleading, I learned from Samira that many of the girls in her first-grade class played cheerleader during gym, herself included. Gym class at Samira's school consists of structured activity and play, and then, at the end of class, a few minutes of "choice time," when the students can choose their own activity. It turned out that during choice time, the girls were choosing cheerleading instead of athletics. I called the school's academic director for an explanation.

My daughter attends a small Quaker school, and for Quakers, individual choice is key to personal growth. They could no more imagine a world without individual choice than they could a week without silent meeting for worship.

But though Quakers encourage the notion of individual choice, they do not believe it should be completely unrestricted. They also believe in the strength of conscience and the power to resist the pressure of popular culture in order to live lives more comfortably grounded in what is simple and necessary and truthful. The girls' cheerleading made the school officials uncomfortable, as it did me.

After I probed other parents and kids about the cheering, I learned something that made me even more uncomfortable: Unbeknownst to the gym teachers, some older boys had been telling girls, especially younger girls, not to play basketball or ride scooters or run relays, because they weren't good enough. The boys told the girls to cheer instead. The girls, of course, are not as skilled as their mothers are in seeing the ways that some boys and men can so easily cast girls to the sidelines. And since cheering is easier and more fun than struggling against boytalk, not to mention wrestling a basketball into a hoop that spirals many feet above their heads, my daughter and her girl pals happily cheered.

Around the same time, Samira brought her American Girl doll to school, dressed to the nines in the new cheerleading outfit, yellow and blue pompoms tied jauntily at the wrist, to the adoration of her girlfriends. During recess that day, though, a boy in her class smashed a rugby ball into the doll's belly. We're not sure why. The boy himself seemed shocked that he had done it, and he did later apologize. He had been among the group of boys telling my daughter and her friends that they weren't good enough athletes to play gym, that they should cheer instead. The classroom teacher saw what happened and led a circle-time conversation about respect. Then, on the after-school playground, another little boy attacked the cheerleading doll, scratching her face. What was it about the cheerleading doll that enraged these boys?

Suddenly, for my daughter, this cheerleading doll now held the memory of boy aggression. Rather than just a cute girl-replica in a short-skirted costume, it became the symbol of standing up to boys, of having a different, girl-based culture and valuing it even when others didn't. After that day, despite my very critical feelings about cheerleading and its improper place in the lives of girls, I tried to take the cheerleading-outfitted doll, and all she represented, more seriously.

At home one weekend, my daughter took her crayon box and large pieces of paper into the living room to make signs. On one, she wrote "American Girl Cheerleaders." She stood her tall American Girl, dressed proudly in the special cheering outfit, next to it. On another large piece of paper she wrote, "American Girl Football Team." Around this sign she placed three shorter American Girls, each dressed in their historic outfits.

"Look, Mom," she called. "They are playing football *and* they are cheerleading. They can do whatever they want, and that makes it all good. They're doing both things, and that makes it okay for some to cheer if they want," she said. "Right, Mom?" Then she asked me for the digital camera so we could snap a photo of the football and cheerleading teams. Which we did.

She approaches these dilemmas perhaps more elegantly than I might, so I have to wonder: Does my history of gender and girliness, of limitation and struggle, matter to her? I know it matters to me. I know it matters to my friends who were in the first cohorts of women at formerly male colleges. I know it mattered to me when at Hicksville Junior High I wanted to take shop, not Home Ec., and my mom had to meet with the principal and persuade him to let me trudge down to the basement twice a week and learn to hammer nails straight and wire electrical cord through old wine bottles to make lamps. The teachers let me do it, but their reluctance was clear (and I still had to take Home Ec.). A few years later, of course, girls and boys were given a choice. Things did change, but it took a long time. How do I help my daughter navigate her own world without revisiting the scars of mine?

My daughter's solutions are so practical. If the problem is that girls are cheerleaders while guys are in the middle of the field squaring off against each other at football, well then, just have girls do both: problem solved. My solutions get lost in the ether of my own memories and the minefield of too much knowledge about the truth of how these things play out in real life. Even today, it is hard to bring up gender inequality in polite society, to mention that only a quick generation has passed—just one, and we're not even half through that one—that blithely assumes that girls can do whatever they want, that promises them they can be astronauts and presidents and corporate CEOs. These gender-equity myths of shooting for the stars don't square with my own life story of leaving the job a PhD prepared me for, turning home because of the hard fact that work life so rarely accommodates motherhood. Are my generation's workplace struggles to be repeated in our daughter's saturation with all things Barbie and Bratz and Hello Kitty? How can any daughter even think about these things when she can be so easily distracted by cheerleading gear available in twenty-four-kid party packs from the Oriental Trading Catalogue, and bullhorns emblazoned on short-sleeved shirts from the Gap and the Children's Place—by a TV girl culture where even though super-teen heroine Kim Possible has a nerdy boy sidekick, she still has to fight evil bad guys, save the world, and be a high school cheerleader too?

When Samira and I talked about the cheerleading-in-school issue after the worst of it had been resolved, she told me in a matter-of-fact voice, "Mom, if you just don't fuss about it, eventually I go on to the next thing." This is true. As she gets older, I can see that some of the girliest stuff is losing a bit of its allure for her—even pink, the most abiding part of the girly-girl package. Last month when we were sorting through the clothes in her closet, she told me I could put all her pink pants, once so beloved, in the giveaway pile. "Girls everywhere love pink," she announces. "But only toddlers—you know, kids younger than me."

As we took my daughter's old clothes from the closet and tossed them into "keep" and "go" piles, I thought of my friend Laura, a feminist theologian of edgy proportion and a thrift-store shopper extraordinaire, who dropped by one day with a pink cashmere sweater culled from the back rack of Village Thrift. "Put it on," she told me. "It's time to get over pink. Real problems for women and girls are out there. Ongoing discrimination. Violence, abuse, shame, and all the rest. But don't blame pink. That's just a color. And it looks good on you."

I thought, too, of how, back in kindergarten, when Samira and her friends were still proudly wearing the color, I was slightly alarmed by the sheer number of girls who showed up for Halloween dressed as frothy pink-clad ballerinas, princesses, butterflies, and fairies. While the kids lined up by class for their Halloween parade around the block, I made a joke with some other parents about the sea of pink.

"Don't worry about it," a mom nearby reassured me. "Look what happens later." As the kindergartners paraded past us, and then the first-graders, the color wheel shifted. Dramatically. The other mom was absolutely right: from second grade on up, the girls, nearly all of them, were wearing black.

"See what happens?" the woman said. "Just when you're ready to die from pink, it's over, and you miss it. It's just a stage."

It's almost the last day of school. First grade has been a good year for Samira, cheerleading controversy aside, and she is happy. She's had a great time with her girlfriends. After a winter of jeans and sweatshirts, she's turned her eye to skirts—especially those skirt-shorts, because when you wear them, you can play on the rainbow climber and your underwear won't show, even when you're hanging upside down, hooked on by only a single knee.

As she gets ready for school in the morning, she brushes her hair with her hands into two ponytails at the front, the rest flowing toward the middle of her back. I come in to check on her, to remind her to brush her teeth and hurry downstairs in time to eat breakfast before heading off to school. I find her standing in front of the full-length mirror in my room, her hands caressing the long ponytails that frame her face. "Aren't they shiny?" she asks me, and then wonders aloud whether she should put the remaining hair in a third, larger ponytail in the back. High up, cheerleader-style.

She's experimenting, of course, as we all are: figuring out who she will be today as she steps out to be in the world, figuring out how to be a girl.

It's a Girl

MARTHA BROCKENBROUGH

I sometimes imagine myself as the unfertilized egg I once was, roosting comfortably in my mother's ovaries until that fateful fall day in 1969, when I popped free from the nest and began my slide into this world, a pearl set free in the primordial soup of life, waiting for the spark that would transform me from cell to living, breathing soul.

It was just my luck, then, that an X chromosome found me first. Why, why, why couldn't it have been a Y? I wondered this for more than thirty years, even before I knew that one small change to the recipe would have meant I'd be a boy. If one of those Y sperm had worked just a little harder, swum a little faster, or bothered to stop for directions along the way, then yes, I could have been a boy. If that had happened, then the world really would have been my oyster. Or so I thought, starting from one of my oldest memories, where I am sitting on the bottom bunk in my brother's room.

It is summer. It is hot. My top is off.

"You're supposed to be wearing a shirt," my brother's friend says. "Girls have to wear shirts."

I look at his bare chest. And I look down at mine. They look the same.

"That's not true." I give him the stink-eye.

"Nope," he says. "Girls have boobs, and they have to wear shirts."

I cupped my flat three-year-old chest with my hands. I didn't feel any boobs there. But just in case he was right about that, I put my shirt back on. I felt sticky in the heat and angry at the injustice of it all. It was one more thing in a growing arsenal of evidence that boys had inherited the better lot in life. In addition to having permission to run around shirtless, they had superior underwear. While mine was plain, theirs was complex, with a hole in the front that could be used for upright peeing, something I tried once with miserable results.

The sitting pee was almost as grave an injustice as sitting on the sidelines while my brothers played baseball. I had to; there was no league for girls back then. And so I sat, while the boys socked their fat mitts and yelled, "heybattaheybattaheybattaHEY," and while they ran backward in the dusty field, tracking a fly ball soaring through the shimmering summer air, I sat on the battered metal bleachers, listening to the mothers chatter. I learned everything I know today about wrapping packages while eavesdropping on one mother, who carefully explained how she folded the edges in on themselves, how she used her nail to make crisp edges, how she liked to hide the tape. I watched another mother reapply her candy-colored lipstick from a well-worn tube, checking out her reflection in her sunglasses. And of course, the mothers swapped recipes.

It all seemed so slow and boring, so unlike the game unfolding on the field below, a game that took so much of my brother's concentration that he would stick out his tongue as he stood, bat in hand, facing down the pitcher. Every time he'd swing, my heart stopped beating and didn't start again until I knew where the ball was going to land—safe in the dirt, or in the hostile mouth of an outfielder's mitt. This was thrilling stuff. It was like a story. There were good guys and bad guys, happy endings and grim defeats. You can't find this sort of thing in a tube of lipstick or a perfectly wrapped box, let alone a Crock-Pot.

I was far too young at the time to understand the lesson I was learning, that the fun and action and recognition I craved most often belonged to the world of boys. I was just six, but I could tell that their world was the one that counted. My doctor was a boy. The president was a boy. And even though he had kind of girly hair, the extremely dreamy Keith Partridge was a boy. I did my best to sneak into their world. I put on my brother's underwear. I wore the neighbor-boys' hand-me-down Toughskins. Like Keith Partridge, I parted my hair in the middle. And it went on from there.

Starting in second grade, I refused to play house with the girls during recess. I joined the gang of boys playing soccer. We'd line up beside the shed, picking teams. Even though I was the smallest, I was good enough that I was never picked last. I played ferociously on the bumpy dirt field, running through mud puddles, jamming my toes into the ball, and hurrying back to class with my face red and sticky with sweat and grime. That year I also joined a swim team, and while I was tiny and got clobbered at meets, I could keep up with anyone during a workout. I could hold my breath longer than anyone, first learning how to swim one length, then two, and then two-and-a-half underwater.

In elementary school, I learned with horror that a period was not just a punctuation mark. In middle school, I made sure I did as many or more chin-ups than the boys, and I hid the thing that was not a punctuation mark from my mother after it first appeared in my stupid, girly panties. In high school I took math and science classes that I hated because I wanted to prove I was as smart as the boys who dominated them. I grew jealous of a girl on the cross-country team after my brother said, "She runs like a guy." I copied her stride, hoping people would notice that I, too, was as good as a boy. And I only watched from afar as my sisters and cousin pored over bride magazines, talking about their future weddings. That stuff seemed like nothing but sugar. It might taste great, but it wasn't good for me. It was girl stuff. Trivial. I was better off without it.

I stayed on this path through college, fuming quietly when the boys who worked for my college newspaper made comments about "incompetent female editors." I worked overtime to prove I was as good—or better—than any boy there, which I was. The same held true at my first newspaper job. I often worked seven days a week to prove this same point. Meanwhile, my boyfriend, who worked at the same place, had less experience, and worked fewer hours, made almost 50 percent more money than I did. So I redoubled my efforts to show the world I could keep up. I started running marathons. I bought my own house and tore out the carpets with my bare hands. This turned out to be a stupid move; the rugs were ancient and grimy, full of all sorts of foul stuff that caused asthma attacks that still plague me every winter. Outside of that same ramshackle little house, I rented a rototiller and tore up my backyard by myself. Then I leveled it and laid sod—finally accepting help from the man I eventually married. This also turned out to be a stupid move. Not the marriage. That's been great. But the grass. Oy. I am allergic to that stuff.

Speaking of marriage. When I first started dating the man I'd hitch my heart to, I explained I did not want to get married, ever. Though I couldn't articulate it, I saw marriage as capitulating to the destiny I had fought. I'd be a wife. A mother. Undeniably a girl. And I would have to choose—either abandoning my children to keep up with my career, or abandoning my ambitions and myself for the vapid, gift-wrapped and lipstick-filled Crock-Pot of motherhood.

But I did it anyway, wearing the one wedding dress in the shop that had no lace, no bows, no demeaning frippery whatsoever. I wore no sexy wedding undergarments, no garter belt, no pricey lotions or perfumes. The only concession I made to being a girl were the B-sized falsies the shop sewed into my dress so that it didn't hang off me like I was an eight-year-old boy. "The Bs are classy," my friend Joel told me as he hung out in the basement room where I got ready with my friends. It took me a minute to realize he was talking about my fake boobs. After the T-shirt lecture my brother's friend had given me all those years ago, it was only the second time in my life a boy had ever talked about my chest.

The wedding was in my parents' backyard. My bridesmaids—my beautiful sisters, good sports, always—wore off-the-rack dresses and sensible, affordable brown shoes.

The bomb of my biological destiny exploded two years later.

Some friends had had a baby, and the first time I held her, a hunger deep inside me awoke. It was as though a false bottom of my heart had given way, opening onto a yawning chasm of desire to have a child.

I got pregnant almost instantly. Days after Adam and I first talked about it, a baby was on the way. I couldn't believe it had happened so fast and that I was going to have to acknowledge the biology I'd been running from since I first grew aware that boys and girls were different. When I'd tell people the news, I couldn't even say "pregnant." I had to say, "I'm having a baby." It was my way of staying active in all of this—active like a man, not passive like the vessel I knew I'd become.

As I barfed my way through the first trimester, I thought about the child blooming inside me and readied myself for the boy I suspected was in there. I studied list after list of boy names. I thought about girl names, too. But the possibility felt so remote that I focused on the ones for boys. Jason? I liked that. Chase? Nice. Griffin? Cool. But was it too weird? Would he get beat up on the playground?

When I was twenty weeks pregnant, I went in for an ultrasound. I had a cold and a terrible cough. My bladder, full to the brim as per my doctor's orders, felt like someone had set a house on it. So I was distracted and anxious to get things over with. I wanted to hurry up and see the teeny penis on the screen that would prove that I was bringing a boy into the world. The baby, as if guided by the invisible hand of god, slipped into perfect viewing position.

"It's a boy!" I said, looking at the small rear end floating like a planet on the screen.

"No it's not," said Adam and the ultrasound tech.

I looked again. They were right. Vagina. Plain as day, looking rather like a hamburger bun in profile.

And then, coughing gently so that I would not wet my pants, I found I could not take my eyes off the screen. I watched the baby, my girl, dance from side to side in my womb. She kept putting her feet together and folding her legs in half, like a diver. Her mouth opened and closed, as though she was trying to tell me something. But what? What would it mean that I was bringing a girl into this world? And how long before I could get her on a baseball team?

That girl is now almost five years old. Despite my best efforts, she has zero interest in baseball. Nor has she a passion for soccer, though she was the only child on the team who knew how to sit crisscross applesauce and smile like a little lady for the team picture. When we watch our local basketball team play, my daughter loves the part when the Sonics dancers bounce onto the court wearing tiny shorts and glittering half-shirts. She weeps if the game goes on past her bedtime. "But I don't want to miss the dancers!"

My daughter has not one, not two, but three princess outfits. She has two "bride hats," as she refers to her veils (one chapel length, one cathedral length, and if she's feeling fancy, she'll wear both at once). As she dreams of the day she will be an actual bride, she regularly identifies potential "groods" and informs me and their mothers of this fact. For Christmas, she asked Santa for two baby dolls. When she is not running around with her shirt pushed up to mimic a Sonics dancer, she has it pushed up so she can breastfeed her rubber spawn.

Despite my expectations and inclinations, my daughter is a girl. A girly, girly, girly girl with long eyelashes, pretty brown eyes, and curls that bounce when she dances, which is often. She does not look at what the boys are doing and think, "They have the life." To her, boys are just potential groods, accessories to her existence who someday will give her the one thing she really wants: a baby of her own.

"I want to be a mother," she tells me every time I ask her what she wants to do with her life.

"But Lucy," I say, "You can be a writer. An artist. A teacher. A pilot. Anything you want."

Nothing doing. She wants to be a mother, eight times over.

"And I will name one of the babies Martha and give it to you," she explains, as if a child named after me—for whom I would then be responsible for the next twenty-one years while I once again crammed my aspirations into a tiny box of child-free time—were the greatest gift in the world.

But in the many times Lucy and I have had this conversation, I am starting to realize she might be right.

In becoming Lucy's mother, I had to learn a great deal. Before then, I'd never taken care of anything besides my dog, whom I loved like she was my sister, so it was no big deal if she ate off my plate, right? I killed all houseplants that crossed my threshold. And I certainly didn't waste time mothering myself. I ate whatever was lying around, as quickly as I could gobble it, so that I could go back to the business of proving I was as good as any man around. This couldn't continue when I had a small child who was utterly dependent on me for her survival, a child I loved more than anything, including my dog, myself, and my own dreams.

When the time came for me to decide whether to go back to my high-profile corporate job or to do something that would allow me to spend more time helping Lucy grow up in a world that favors those with a penis, I let go of the fancy job. I watched my daughter unfold like a flower before my eyes, and in the free time I could make for myself, I became the one thing I'd really wanted to be, besides a boy.

I became a writer. This is something one cannot do without exploring the darkest, dirtiest holes that tunnel through the heart and mind. As I crawled through those sometimes miserable spaces, getting familiar with the hatred I'd felt about the fact that I was born a girl and would never rule the world, I realized something else. I stopped looking at the world as though it were an oyster.

For one thing, I observed, I never liked oysters. They taste terrible. And for another thing, no matter what I'd been paid to do it, I had managed to do everything the boys had done, and I'd done something more: given birth to a child. My daughter, my pearl.

And not just one. Exactly three and a half years after Lucy arrived, I had another—a second daughter, very different from the first. Unlike Lucy, Alice doesn't need to be held all the time. She gets furious if I try to help her climb the stairs. When she taught herself to walk, she concentrated so fiercely, her tongue stuck out, not unlike the way my brother's did when he held a baseball bat over his shoulder.

So I might get my baseball player after all, along with my princess. Either way, I do not care. I am just thrilled to be there, watching them and loving them, feeling infinitely grateful for the X chromosome that allowed me to give them life, as my mother gave me life, and as her mother did before hers, like a string of pearls stretching backward in time to the first mother of us all, a woman who probably never gave a moment's thought to whether she was as good as the men, so long as her children were alive.

And so this is my life now. Becoming a mother, having a girl, has helped me love the girl I am. I may no longer have the prestige, the power, or the money that comes from succeeding in the boy's world. But I am a mother. A mother of daughters. And this is more.

ON BEAUTY AND
A DAUGHTER

On Being Barbie

JENNY
BLOCK

My daughter plays with Barbies, and I'm starting to look like one. I can't help but wonder—is this a bad thing?

You see, I believe I am teaching her all the right stuff. That she should respect people and their differences. That neither beauty nor weight speaks to the quality of a person's soul. That kindness and intelligence are the virtues toward which everyone should strive.

But I also have quite a few fashion magazines lying around. And I do take an inordinate amount of pride in my appearance.

And, well, when things aren't looking quite the way I would like, I've had no problem with visiting a plastic surgeon—three times.

In 1991, well before I was married or had a child, I had my first plastic surgery, a nose job. My reason for doing it was simple and not the least bit profound: I hated my nose.

I had first asked my parents for the surgery in 1986, for my sixteenth birthday. They, of course, would hear none of it. I whined, I pleaded—I begged, in fact—but my mother refused. "You're beautiful," she told me. "You have to say that," I replied, "you're my mom!" But the answer was no.

Five years later, I had it done. I didn't preselect some movie star nose, I just asked Dr. Williams to give me the kind of nose that would seem plausible—normal—on my face. And he did. Most people don't even notice, though it's not a fact I try to hide. I've been accused of being narcissistic for having the surgery. But the nose job actually made me less focused on my looks. In a way, my new nose makes me less noticeable, which was precisely what I wanted.

My daughter is three. She watches me get dressed in the morning. One day she sees me turn sideways to the mirror and smooth down the fabric on the back of my pants.

"What are you looking at, Mommy?" she asks.

"Just checking," I say.

"What are you checking?" she asks.

I feel like I did when I was seventeen, going to the drugstore to buy condoms for the first time. "May I help you?" the clerk had asked. I knew exactly what I wanted to say, but my head swam with all of the implications that would stick the moment I opened my mouth. Fifteen years later, I am again at a loss for words. Not because I don't know what I want to say. But because I don't want to be the person that telling the truth will surely imply I am. So I lie.

"Where are the light bulbs?" I asked the clerk back then, instead of asking for the condoms.

"I'm just checking to make sure my pants are ironed nicely," I answer my daughter now, instead of telling her that I'm checking out my ass to make sure I don't look fat.

"Aisle two," the clerk had answered.

"They'll get wrinkly when you sit on your bum anyway," my daughter tells me.

My first fib put me in danger. At least, it had the potential to, if I had proceeded to have sex with my boyfriend without procuring the items in question.

But my second fib puts both myself and my daughter in danger. If I fudge the truth, she is in danger of walking into the world unprepared for its harsh, "weightist," looks-obsessed realities; in danger of becoming a looks-obsessed, "weightist" woman herself; or worse, in danger of suffering from eating disorders or a life filled with inevitable failures as she seeks perfection that only airbrushing brings. And by fudging the truth, I, of course, am in danger of being a liar. I am in danger of simply mouthing the words I think reflect the person I should be if I am to raise a healthy, strong, happy, self-confident daughter, rather than reflecting the person I really am.

Hence my quandary.

If I tell my daughter the truth about this, she will know that I think it is good to be thin and that I think that being fashionable is important. She will know that I watch what I eat, closely, and that I spend more on shoes than her father, my husband, will ever realize.

She will know that I am shallow.

Adolescent angst about my nose aside, I have always been comfortable with, and in, my body. As an adult, I worked in the theater, I took on modeling jobs, I had doting lovers. I did not obsess about the way I looked.

Then, once I was married, I got pregnant.

I gained so much weight that even after I lost it, post-baby, I was left with a mass of sagging skin and torn abdominal muscles. All of a sudden, my body was getting in my way. I couldn't fit into my clothes. I wore painful, constricting undergarments that caused me stomach problems. Smiling waitresses in restaurants and well-meaning friends at parties asked me when I was due. Quite honestly, I couldn't take it.

A year after my daughter was born, I had my second plastic surgery.

The surgeon cut off the extra skin, sucked out the excess fat, and sewed my muscles back together. I had my old stomach back. It felt like coming home.

You see, despite what some people think, I wasn't ever trying to be someone else. I was simply trying to get back to myself.

My daughter is five. I am drying my hair in the bathroom, naked, save for my underwear. I am bent forward, drying my hair upside down. As I switch the dryer off, I hear a little voice say, "You look just like a cow, Mommy."

"What?" I laugh, straightening up.

"Not now. But bend over," she says. So I do. "See." She points to my breasts. "You're like a cow."

My once-32D breasts, now empty Bs, dangle. She is right, verbalizing what I have been thinking since I stopped breastfeeding her.

I know just the guy to talk to.

"Well, I'll tell you the truth," Dr. DeWire tells me at my first consult. "You're not a particularly good candidate. You're asymmetrical. Your skin's all stretched out as far as it can take it. I don't know," he says, weighing my breasts in his hands. "And I see you brought a bunch of pictures?"

"Yes."

"No need," he tells me. "I'll give you what your frame calls for. I'll do a lift and put in the implant size that works. Think about it, though. You won't look seventeen again."

And I do think about it. A lot. I think about the risks. The pain. The time. The expense. The reasons why I really want to do it. But more than anything, I think about Hannah. My nose was done before she was born. My stomach was done before she was old enough to notice the difference. But my breasts would be done when she was five, and I wonder about what she would think; how much she would understand; what, if anything, I should tell her.

After much deliberation, I decide to have the surgery—not because I have everything figured out, but because I make a deal with myself: If I have the surgery, I will commit myself to a lifelong dialogue with Hannah. I will always tell Hannah the truth, in age-appropriate ways, and I will be there to help her work through just what all of it meant and what all of it continues to mean—plastic surgery, "weightism," our national virgin/whore complex, the mystery of beauty, all of it.

Deciding to have surgery was the right decision for me—every time. I am very happy with my new nose, my new stomach, my new breasts. But having had plastic surgery, particularly breast implants, forces me to have to prove sometimes who I really am. Looking like Barbie grants me all the Barbie privileges—never waiting in line, never paying a bar tab, never wanting for a cab or a dance partner. But of course the price I pay for resembling a toy is that I often have to deal with being treated like a toy. There are men who assume I'm an airhead, and there are women who assume I'm a bitch. But there's nothing I enjoy more than surprising a man with how smart and witty I am, or disarming a woman with my friendliness and generosity. I've always had an able brain and an engaging personality. Plastic surgery didn't remove that.

I wanted to look a certain way, and people treat me certain ways because of that. All I can say is that this is who I am. Some people may dislike me because of those decisions, but I far prefer that to disliking myself.

It's all about choices. It's all about balance. It's all about awareness. And that—all of that—is what I will tell Hannah about this issue and the many others she will face. That is what I will tell her now, and that's what I will tell her for as long as she continues to look to me to understand the world and her place in it.

Barbies, beauty, weight, plastic surgery—I don't have all the right answers. But I don't think answers are what I owe to Hannah. What I owe her is open and intelligent discussions about these issues. What I owe her is the opportunity to think, to learn, and to at least try to understand.

My daughter is six. "When am I going to get those?" she asks, pointing to my breasts. Several answers flash through my head. *When you go through puberty. When you're a teenager. When you can afford them.*

"Well, Mommy?" she asks again.

"When you're bigger," I say.

"Oh," she replies, satisfied for now.

But I know I'm not going to be able to get away with that much longer. This is just the beginning of what is sure to be a lengthy and ongoing conversation—one that won't always be pretty.

But, you know, that's just fine with me.

The Food Rules

ANN
DOUGLAS

The first time I seriously freaked out about what my daughter was eating, I was barely halfway through my pregnancy with her.

It was 1988, and thinking about food was something I was good at. Really good at. In fact, just the year before, I'd managed to achieve my goal weight through Weight Watchers by analyzing every tablespoon or ounce of food that made it onto my plate and hence into my stomach. It took me six months to shed the extra fifty-four pounds I'd been carrying around—six months of weighing bagels and measuring the amount of cream that went into my morning coffee. Of course, that time I had a mission—something I'd been lacking every other time I'd ever joined Weight Watchers in the past: motherhood. I wanted to maximize my fertility—and fast. Needless to say, I didn't manage to stay at my goal weight very long. Three weeks, to be exact.

So there I was, five months pregnant, sitting in a movie theater with my husband and helping him finish off a bucket of buttered popcorn. I reached over and grabbed a swig of whatever he was drinking to wash down some of the butter and salt, only to realize in horror that I had ingested diet cola. *Caffeinated, artificially sweetened cola*—a beverage that the pregnancy book gurus of the day considered to be only marginally better than cigarettes, alcohol, or crack cocaine.

My panic was such that I momentarily considered bolting to the bathroom and forcing myself to vomit up the noxious liquid—though I had a feeling that do-it-yourself puking was similarly frowned upon by the pregnancy-book authors in question. (Unfortunately, I'd neglected to bring my book to the movie theater, so I had no way of knowing for sure.) I'm not sure what the rest of the movie was about, since from that point on I basically created a movie in my head called *So You Think You're Fit for Motherhood, Ha!* Maybe you've caught previews for that particular flick at various times, too.

But the patron saint of expectant mothers must have been looking out for me that night, because despite my nutritional faux pas, my 8.5-pound, blue-eyed baby girl was born in perfectly good health a few months later, showing no obvious aftereffects from my moment of reckless abandon. True, as a newborn she was colicky for a few hours each evening, and I did wonder if perhaps the colic could be payback for my momentary sur- render to that artificial sweetener and caffeine cocktail. But breastfeeding helped us to get through those tough nights—and it also took the worry out of trying to figure out how much to feed my baby. All I needed to do was to offer her the breast when she was hungry and stop feeding her when she decided she'd had enough to eat. It was as simple as that. I found this reassuring, as I was concerned about feeding: Family legend had it that I had gone from being a scrawny five-pound, thirteen-ounce newborn to a chubby child because my parents had offered me a bottle every time I cried. This was, evidently, a bad thing. After hearing that story repeated at frequent intervals throughout my entire life, and after wrestling with my own weight issues growing up, I was determined to get feeding right with my child.

Once she started on solids, I tried to maintain my low-key approach. I followed the infant feeding rules to the letter, introducing solids in just the right order and at just the right intervals, all the while carefully steering clear of the long list of foods that were taboo. (If I was going to end up in the Bad Mommies Club, it wasn't going to be on account of a tablespoon of honey.) When my baby girl suddenly morphed into a toddler and went on food strikes or through food jags, or when she decided to play with her food rather than eating it, I refused to get fazed by what was—or wasn't— going into her mouth. Then my toddler morphed into a preschooler, and my preschooler morphed into a kindergartner and then a grade-schooler, and the stakes kept getting higher and higher. Suddenly food wasn't just between my daughter and me. My daughter was hanging out in the world of little girls—girls in third grade who dressed like teenagers and who cared about the size of one another's bellies and who asked one another whether or not they should be on diets. My daughter started wondering if she was fat—and I started worrying how many points she was losing on the playground for having a plus-sized mom.

I'd had fantasies during my pregnancy with my daughter that I would go back to my Weight Watchers goal weight right after I gave birth, or maybe after doing the bizarro exercises that always seemed to be tucked away in the final chapter of any self-respecting pregnancy book. But when you gain fifty-four pounds during your pregnancy (the exact amount of weight I had lost at Weight Watchers the previous year), you're either going to have to give birth to one heck of a big baby—or babies—in order to morph back into your pre-pregnancy self, or you're going to have to do an awful lot of postbaby tummy crunches. I did neither. Instead, I got pregnant again, giving birth to my second baby nineteen months after delivering the first—and going for round number three another nineteen months after that. With each pregnancy, I added a few more pounds.

It wasn't until my daughter was in seventh grade—after I had given birth to baby number four—that I managed to make serious inroads with my weight problem, dropping seventy-four pounds. I lost the weight by walking with a friend when I had time and eating moderately. I didn't discuss my weight loss in front of my daughter because I didn't want her to get the message that dieting was "normal" behavior for moms—even though I obviously had weight to lose. She noticed my weight loss anyway and one day handed me a card: "Congratulations! Just don't get anorexic." It struck me as an odd comment at the time, but I assumed she was simply making note of the fact that a significant percentage of her mother had disappeared. And we had talked about the dangers of eating disorders, and I was sure she was learning about them in health class too. So I put the card aside without worrying too much. Later, her words would haunt me.

As I worked on my own body issues, my daughter—who had refused to wear any clothes with buttons, lace, or anything "itchy" right from day one—began applying her increasingly discriminating tastes to the world of food. Pizza, which she had loved as a toddler, now topped the list of most-hated foods—a list that seemed to be growing by the day. Going out for dinner as a family became a nightmare by the time she started junior high. Most family restaurants didn't carry a single item that was either suitable or cooked the way she liked it. She fared only marginally better at home since she hated most dinners, period.

I noticed this, but I also noticed that while my daughter was busy developing a set of "food rules" for herself that would have made some of the most stringent diet plans read like a trip to the dessert buffet, she was also trying to figure out where she fit into the Land of the Britneys, the Xtinas, the pop-starlets who seemed to be determined to outsex one another on MTV. My own generation had its pressures—who among us didn't hope to morph into some glamorous creature bearing at least a fleeting resemblance to Farrah Fawcett, the TV starlet whose swimsuit picture was the stuff of schoolboy fantasies when I was in high school? But back then I could at least take solace in the fact that I was still a work in progress: Farrah was a woman, while I was barely in need of a training bra. Teenage girls of my daughter's generation, however, are pressured to compete with a never-ending parade of impossibly perfect teenagers.

So maybe I shouldn't have been surprised on that late June evening during my daughter's eighth-grade year when I was looking in her closet and I came across a jumbo-sized candy container filled with vomit. Her room had developed a low-level odor that she apparently didn't even notice anymore. I had insisted that she clean her room, but I was keeping her company because she seemed like she could use some moral support. Besides, once everything was off the floor and out of the closet, I wanted to get out the spray cleaners and tackle that smell.

I ventured into the closet and started pulling out all the random paraphernalia that my daughter had crammed inside her closet. Then I hit the mother lode.

"What's this?" I asked as I held up the see-through container of sloshing pinkish liquid.

"That should be obvious," she replied matter-of-factly.

Finding that container threw my parenting equilibrium out of whack.

I no longer knew how to speak the language of food with my daughter. So I switched into research mode. I wanted to know why that container had ended up in my daughter's closet. I went online and hit both the official eating disorder websites and the pro–eating disorder websites in order to get some insights into what was going on inside my daughter's head.

The pro–eating disorder websites are both a freaked-out parent's worst nightmare and a fact-hungry parent's nirvana—the sources of nitty-gritty information you won't find anywhere else, like tips on mastering the silent puke (flush twice, do it in the shower, mask the sounds with a cough). My trip to the eating disorder underworld helped me to understand the thought processes that may have led my daughter to conclude that an in-room vomitorium worked much better than making treks to upchuck in the family bathroom upstairs (put on some music, close the door, and voilà, no one can hear you puke).

My daughter began treatment through the local eating disorder clinic. She wasn't there because she wanted to be there. She didn't think she had a problem. She was there because we wanted her to go. "Let us worry about how much your daughter is eating," our daughter's counselor stressed. "You just focus on being her parents."

It's hard to play it cool when every spoon in the house is missing and you're not sure whether they've been recruited as tools in a binge or a purge—or both. And finding out that low-fat cream cheese was no longer low-fat enough for her—or discovering that the $7 bag of frozen blueberries she had asked for had been vomited up just moments after being swallowed down—could be crazy-making. At times I felt like I'd gone back in time to when I was a brand new mom, cranking up the volume on the baby monitor so that I could hear my daughter's every movement in an effort to keep her safe, as if vigilance on my part would guarantee her wellbeing.

That kind of vigilance doesn't come without a price—the price being mother burnout. Just as I had become totally immersed in my daughter's rising and falling moods when she was an infant, I found myself getting dragged on the eating-disorder rollercoaster ride too—a ride that was largely determined by how hungry she was (if she was hungry, she was edgy as hell), what she'd pumped into her body to ramp up her metabolism or to purge her body of food (think caffeine, ephedrine, and laxatives), how much sleep she'd had the night before (midnight raids on the fridge and the subsequent purges inevitably cut into your dreamtime), and how volatile she was at any given moment. Oh, yeah—and because we're talking about a teenager here, you can also add hormones, attitude, and "normal" teenage angst to the equation. It made for a rather combustible mix.

As any parent who has walked this path can tell you, coping with a colicky infant is a cakewalk compared to dealing with the mercurial mood swings of a teenager with an eating disorder. Though it doesn't feel like it in the moment, colic is a limited-time offer. You only have to weather that particular emotional storm for a matter of weeks or months, and you and your baby will be just fine once it passes. When your teenager has an eating disorder, the experts and the books don't offer the same reassuring words. The experts don't know when—or if—your child is going to get better, or how her long-term health will be affected. And ultimately you have to relearn the lesson that you learned back in your child's baby days: that your child's food choices are entirely her own. Whether a bite of food goes in at all or stays down for longer that a minute or two is entirely out of your control. It's only once you surrender that control—and realize that you never had that control in the first place—that you can regain anything that even remotely resembles peace of mind.

And then there's that piece about forgiving yourself—the toughest part for most of us parents. I had to learn to forgive myself for passing along genes that may have contributed to my daughter's eating disorder, for being a less-than-perfect parent, and for not being able to protect my daughter from a culture that sends girls some seriously messed up messages about food and what it means to look good and feel good about yourself.

But I also learned that just as certain pregnancy books like to overdo it with the doom-and-gloom forecasts, some of the eating disorder materials aimed at parents paint the situation as hopeless when that may not actually be the case. Now, with therapy and time and family support, my daughter's world no longer revolves around food to the extent it once did.

When I picked my daughter up from her part-time job a few nights ago, she was in tears. She had just found out that she and some of the other part-timers were being let go. So much for that first job she'd been so proud about landing a few weeks earlier.

"Can we pick up some bread?" my daughter asked. "I don't think we have any left at home."

I pulled over at a local variety store and picked up a loaf of ultra-squishy white bread—my daughter's favorite kind. Then I lingered in front of the ice cream freezer. Would buying my daughter a tub of ice cream be the right or wrong thing to do? On the one hand, it might be the trigger for a binge. On the other hand, it could be a nurturing thing to do, to cushion her pain with some sweetness.

What would other mothers do? I asked myself, trying to conjure up some all-knowing June Cleaver or Carol Brady mother-figure who would instinctually know whether buying the ice cream was the right or wrong thing. But then again, those two had never had a bulimic child to grocery shop for—at least not based on the *Leave It to Beaver* and *Brady Bunch* episodes I'd manage to catch.

In the end, I decided to err on the side of the ice cream. After all, if it's okay to nurture your best friend with chocolate when the occasion calls for it, why can't you toss a bit of creamy vanilla ice cream your teenage daughter's way when she's just been shafted by Big Retail? Has society sent us so many mixed messages about food that we've lost our comfort level with good old-fashioned comfort foods?

I'm glad I took that chance—that I trusted my mothering instincts and bought that tub of ice cream even though I was worried I might be breaking one of the "food rules." Not only did buying the sweet treat allow my daughter to partake in that time-honored female tradition known as ice cream therapy, it served as a token of faith that I believed that the worst of her eating disorder was behind her. ("Isn't it great that I can eat normally now?" she said as she placed her ice cream bowl into the dishwasher.)

Sometimes you've just got to trust your instincts—your *gut instincts*—when your daughter is concerned.

Feeling Is First:
On Beauty and a Daughter

GWENDOLEN
GROSS

I appreciate beauty along with the best of 'em. I appreciate the appreciation of beauty as well, but when the bearer of said beauty is one of my children, it makes me wonder about the impact of hearing, "Oh my god, look at those curls! Do you see her, Bob? Do you see that little girl? She looks just like a doll!"

They know she is not a doll, but they say it anyway; we hear it, I exaggerate not, at least four times weekly. But there is nothing plastic about Clare. She likes to eat spaghetti with her fingers, she enjoys galloping in mud puddles, she has temper tantrums, and her socks most definitely are not just painted on. I know she knows she's not a doll, but I hope to show her the grand variety and scope of beauty in the world.

When her beauty is remarked upon, I try to tell her, "Sweetheart, you know what's beautiful? Those new leaves on the maple tree—and the way blue and yellow mix and make green."

"And me," she says, not asking.

"Right. You know when you're beautiful? When you say thank you.

You're beautiful when you share and you're beautiful when you look at the grape hyacinths with me and you're beautiful when you go shopping and use the little cart and don't get upset because we can only get a dozen fruit leathers, not more."

"And when I wear my pink hat," she says, but I hope she gets the general idea.

I have just finished assembling sixteen pink poodle paper cone hats for Clare's third birthday. Unlike her brother, who had parties with a few family friends and didn't care about themes until he reached the half-decade mark (and then asked: "May I have an equation on my cake?"), my daughter was thrilled to pick out her party hats, plates, cups, spoons, goodie-bags, and general paraphernalia from the online catalogue of birthday madness. I knew she wanted doggies, but I didn't realize the passionate draw of pink poodles in particular. "My friends will all come! The pink poodles will make them laugh!" she says.

My daughter started going to school as a toddler. I felt guilty, of course, but in that mildly tempered way of second-child parenting: You have a mammoth stomachache, but you don't actually throw up in your minivan on the drive to work. It took a few weeks for her to settle in, but I knew the center, and her teachers were wonderful, especially Tracy, who sang to her and sat with her and understood that she may have looked dainty, but there was a serious, clever, and highly silly person under that mop of Shirley Temple hair.

Now, in her second year of school, she's a veteran. We used to hear a lot from her about who pushed whom and who had a time out and who wore a watch to school—now we hear about special weird noises she makes only with Darren and who is using the potty and how best friends stay best friends even when they are grownups and sit in the front seat of the van and chew gum without swallowing. And we hear about birthday parties—the one at Build-a-Bear, the dancing one, the backyard one, and hers, which will be *very, very beautiful.*

I have some reservations about dwelling on beauty. Of course I tell my daughter she's adorable, but I also make sure she knows how smart she is—and she is, full of observations about people that astonish me. "That man is going home," she said peering into a Ford at a stoplight. "Because he has his smiling eyes on." When we read a doggie alphabet book, she is quite serious, studying. At the end, she tells me, "But Doggie got a bug bite on his nose. Is he all better, or does he need a Band-Aid?" My son was obsessed with other things at this age, so the focus on feelings is a new world of preschooler parenting for me. Her brother is amazing with numbers and not so good at reading people, though he's trying. Clare may have phenomenal math skills too, I don't know yet; but she's definitely an empath. Feeling is first for her. I worry that her beauty, and her concern for others' feelings, will attract unwanted attention, but I'll do my best, I'll be vigilant on her behalf.

We go to the ice cream store to pick up Clare's purple and pink butterfly cake. Standing in the line, a grandmother says to her granddaughter of seven or eight, "Oh, honey, look at that cute little girl!"

Clare has always been aware of attention—she notices the woman noticing and asks me to pick her up. It isn't that she minds meeting people, and when I tell people she's shy, I know I don't mean that, exactly. For people who matter, friends who want to really know her, I try to explain, "She'd rather approach than be approached." And I suppose most of us feel that way, though we each have different-sized universes of personal space. Do fame-seekers actually want to be known all the time at first, or is it the idea of attention, rather than the specifics of it, that's appealing? Of course we want attention—we just want to be in control of it.

"What a cutie!" The grandma reaches out to touch Clare's curls, and Clare ducks her head into me but smiles.

The granddaughter pulls her grandmother's hand, points toward the mix-ins. I can practically see her thinking, "Geez, Grandma, what'm I? A hunchback? What happened to my cuteness?"

I wanted to tell this grandmother: Give your own granddaughter a squeeze; she's plenty cute and she needs to hear it now—and in a year, and when she's thirteen and feels like she can't wear bikinis that show off her baby belly. When she's fifteen and has temporarily terrible skin and too-long limbs and colored braces that look worse than the metal kind. I vow to remember to tell Clare how beautiful she is—and not just beautiful, but cute—despite my reservations about dwelling on appearances.

But as she has grown, the reach-out-and-touch impulse of the strangers around her hasn't diminished, it has increased. People want to touch her hair, shake her hand. I know that impulse: We want to commune with cute animals, even if we know they might bite. I remember looking at toddlers—girls in particular—when I was thinking about diving into the deep lake of parenthood myself. They were *so cute*. They were so innocent. I suppose they reminded me of my own girlhood sense of power and powerlessness combined. Or maybe that's too philosophical—maybe cute is just cute.

Either way, I want to teach her both to be friendly and to protect herself, to respect all her talents and features worthy of attention—not just physical beauty, which may remain or may change as she does, but her ideas, her questions, and the empathy that both draws her to people and inspires her to hide. Perhaps that is what will keep her safe—once she understands her own desires (for attention, for privacy), and once she has names for the emotions she clearly recognizes in others (kindness, interest, jealousy, greed), she can approach or avoid without need for parental protection.

It's just that she's always received this attention, and maybe always will, and that will have some impact. Hopefully good. Hopefully she will enjoy the interest and also understand what is valuable—what is casual consideration and what is closeness, the difference between looking at art and making it. Two acts of attention; two ways of being, communicating.

"Mama," she says. "That girl is going to get M&Ms in her ice cream!" Luckily, she's noticing what's really important.

The party is a huge success. There are hardly any tantrums, just a room full of gymnastics equipment and wild, ecstatic almost-or-just three-year-olds swinging, bouncing on the trampolines, and grinning at each other in shared experience. They mingle in the giant tunnels, roll down the padded slides together. They're talking, but mostly they're just doing, reveling in their bodies' relatively new abilities to explore space. They are all beautiful, running, rolling. They hug each other, thrilled to be together outside of school. There are spontaneous kisses. Sure, there are a few tears when someone else tries to blow out the candles on Clare's cake, when one girl doesn't get the exact pink flower she wants; but mostly, it's motion, screaming with pleasure, then pizza, cake, and a temporary paralysis due to exhaustion in the car on the way home.

"It can't be over," says Clare, "because we haven't had all of the fun yet."

That night in the bathtub, washing off the frosting and pizza sauce, Clare is playing with her princesses. One is named after Clare, the second after her best friend, Maddie, and I ask about the third, who is technically Snow White.

"What is her name?"

Clare plunges her under the bubbles. "She's a really really good diver," she says. "She likes to hold her breath."

"What's her name?" I ask again.

"She's *so beautiful*, and she likes her blue dress," she says. Then she names the biggest boy in her class. "Yep. She's *so beautiful*, and her name's Robby."

She's right, and I know it will be okay; I know she has an inkling of what beauty really is.

Breasts: A Collage

**RACHEL
HALL**

I.

I'm in the women's shower room at the university pool. At six or seven, I'm all gangly arms and legs, long brown hair—of which I'm exceptionally proud. In the pool, I'm my father's girl—swimming laps alongside him, doing fancy turns at the wall, my braids slapping my back as I swoosh and start for the other side, the black lap lines wobbling beneath me as I swim. Do I like the buzz of exertion in my arms and legs, or is it my father's rare approval, his obvious pleasure in my endurance, that I like?

In the shower, it's all women. I watch the soap and shampoo crest and foam on the green tile floor, swirl down the drain. I'm unaware of the women's conversations as they bathe, though behind me I can hear lockers slamming, shouts echoing. My mother is talking with another faculty wife, Mrs. Goodman, and undoing my braids. "Stand still," she says. She'd like me to get a nice short haircut like her own, but this won't happen for many years still. She shampoos my hair, scrubbing my scalp brusquely. I look up at Mrs. Goodman, at her naked breasts. They are different from my mother's—wider, with tiny nipples like raisins. I look around at the other breasts in the shower. Some are large and bobbly. Others look like triangles when their owners bend to soap themselves. Some are topped with pink nipples, while others are plum-colored, brown. Still others are all nipple with only the slightest puff of flesh. They're as different as noses, I think in an abstracted way. This observation from the land of women has nothing to do with me.

II.

The other girls are the worst: Andrea Miles, Marie Keath, Margaret Epple. They run up to me, to each other, and grab at the nipple, where it's most tender, and twist. "Mosquito bites!" they shriek, or "Itty-bitty titties!" On the playground or at gym, they snap bra straps, and the smacking sound seems thunderous, booming. All summer, I've hunched my shoulders, worn thick cardigans despite the Midwestern heat and humidity. In addition to breasts, which are tiny but visible, there are other horrors too humiliating to speak of. My hair, once smooth and glossy, kinks up, frizzes around my face, and can't be tamed with barrettes or headbands.

And now my mother and I have come downtown to buy my first bra. This is downtown Columbia, Missouri, before the advent of the mall, in the year of America's bicentennial. The fire hydrants have been painted to look like Revolutionary War soldiers. In a couple years, after the mall comes, downtown will falter and then fail, but right now it's where all the action is. My mother drives past the bead store, past the deli where my friends and I can make a bag of chips last hours. Once she parks, I slink from our station wagon into the store called Pranges Intimate Apparel.

Is the carpet really a plush purple? The walls lime green? This is how I remember it—everything too bright, garish—including the saleswoman's teased red hair, her long crimson nails. The store is packed with racks of bras and panties in all colors. I can't move without knocking one off. This might be laughable if it weren't excruciating, if I weren't twelve, sweating in my navy blue cardigan.

My mother explains our business, and suddenly I'm in the dressing room with the saleswoman. "Turn around, dahlink," she says. Could she really have an accent like Zsa Zsa Gabor? Is she for real? When I don't move, she spins me around, her nails sharp through my clothes. "Shirt off," she says, and I understand: She isn't leaving. Where's my mother? I'm furious with her for not preparing me for this, for having made me female and thus put me in this horrible, compromised position. I peel off my clothing, make myself as small as possible, and try to pretend I'm not here, half-naked with a stranger. The saleslady fastens the bra for me with a competent snap. "You vant to buy so you use the middle set of hooks," she explains. She adjusts the shoulder straps. "Bend over," she says, demonstrating how I should bend from the waist so my flesh will fill the bra's cups.

When I stand again, she's looking at my chest. "Too big," she says. "You see those puckers?"

I nod. She hands me another bra, and we repeat the exercise until I have one that fits. It is white and plain, a virginal rosebud stitched in the V between the cups. I plan to remove the bud immediately when we get home.

We leave the store with the bras in a hot-pink and white striped bag bearing the shop's name in loopy script. I make my mother carry it in case we see someone I know. In our boat of a car, I slide down in the seat and hug my arms around my treacherous chest.

Many years later, when my mother's left breast has been removed and sloppy stitches traverse her chest, I'll overhear a mother and her young daughter shopping for bras in the department store dressing room next to me, and I'll have to leave, to rush out quickly without making a purchase.

III.
Of the many slang words for breasts, an alarming number are vehicular. Headlights, for instance, or Cadillacs, hubcaps, grillwork, B-52s, torpedos, front-end alignment, tanks, car waxers, airbags, battleships, bumpers. It's interesting too, though less surprising, that there are so many food references: apples, avocados, peaches, plums, cantaloupes, coconuts, guavas, funnel cakes, Ho-Hos, hotcakes, loaves, jugs, lollies, brisket. Grocery shopping becomes an erotic affair! The terms love lumps, lulas, titties, teetees, tatas, and naynays rely on a comforting alliteration—part baby talk, part poetry. Perhaps these comprise the language of love? My personal favorite is a term I came across online: lost sheep. As if the rest of the flock were elsewhere. Where? I think of Little Bo Peep in a ruffled petticoat and bonnet, a beribboned staff in her hand. Or of Heidi, breathing in the clear mountain air.

IV.
I nurse everywhere—on park benches, in restaurants, on planes, in the car (both stationary and moving), in the bookstore, in my sleep or near sleep (who sleeps anymore, really?). I nurse in front of anyone. Strangers, mother, father, brother, friends, former students. I've bought and been given several nursing shirts—cotton numbers with convenient open-

ings and flaps—but it turns out it's easier to lift a regular shirt. I've been instructed how to drape myself and the baby with a blanket to avoid stares, but all that cloth gets in the way. Instead of hiding us, the blanket flags us: *What's going on under there, lady?* I don't have time for any of this subterfuge anyway. When my girl wants to nurse, I have to move fast. I can tell when she's starting to get hungry because she makes these desperate panting noises—like a tiny addict. She is all fierce need. Am I drug or pusher? Both. I am everything, her whole world.

One night when she is about six weeks old, she doesn't wake to nurse. I try to leap up, but pain pins me to the bed. My breasts, full of milk, are too heavy. Sandbags. I have to lift them with both hands, carry them as I check on my daughter, sleeping peacefully in her bassinet. Her eyes quiver under her lids, her lips purse. She dreams of milk.

And then, as suddenly as they began, our public-nursing days are over. My girl wants quiet. She wants me alone. If my husband enters the room and tries to talk, she pulls off the nipple and begins to wail, outraged. If I try to read, she smacks the book out of my way, the mere turning of pages a disturbance she can't abide. It's just the two of us now, all my other loves banished. Sometimes when she nurses, she looks up at me and smiles, her small hand reaching up and patting my breast.

I like it here. I'm good at this, surprisingly good. Awash with milk, my mind goes blank. My nipples don't crack or bleed. My breasts are bountiful. I love even the breastfeeding words—"rooting," for the baby's purposeful turning and nuzzling; the vaguely nautical "latching on," for the deep kiss at the nipple which summons the milk; "let down," for the pinch at my nipple just before the milk streams out. I contemplate career change: lactation consultant, wet nurse . . . for surely the life of the mind is overrated.

V.

Over my mother's bed hangs a portrait. In it, she sits in a rocking chair, looking down at me, a swaddled infant at her breast. She is younger than I am now—her face lovely and smooth, her hair dark, mouth red and lip-sticked. When I nurse my daughter, the nightlight in her room casts us in shadow. My bent head and the slats on the rocker appear on the wall and ceiling and remind me of the painting. I feel close to my mother, as if my rocking—like her rocking before—has brought us near. More than that, I forget I'm the mother here, not the child.

My mother breastfed me for a year, a slightly radical thing to do in the early 1960s, when the 1950s preoccupation with science and hygiene still held sway. "It was wonderful," she says of nursing. "Nobody told me how wonderful it would be."

Now, however, a routine mammogram has revealed suspicious cells in her breast. I'm in my daughter's room, rocking and nursing, when my mother calls with the biopsy results. We've been expecting her call, alternating between hope and dread. I hear my husband in the hallway. "Oh, no," he says. "I'm sorry. No, no, I'll tell her."

My arms are full of my nursing baby, so I can't wipe my tears. They roll down my cheeks, landing on my daughter, who nurses on, sweaty with sleep.

It's my mother's left breast; the breast that babies tend to favor because they can hear the thump of their mother's heartbeat, as they did in the womb.

We are born nostalgic, it seems, always yearning for what has passed.

In the next weeks and months I will learn things that I never wanted to know, this unlovely vocabulary—metastisis, ductal carcinoma in situ, lumpectomy, multi-foci, cytoxin, aridimex, tamoxifen. I will learn that insurance companies pay for breast reconstructions because it is believed to help women to move on, to recover. A nipple for the reconstructed breast can be tattooed on or fashioned from the tissue of the labia. Many women who opt for reconstruction forgo the nipple, which would feel no sensation anyway. Is a breast without a nipple a breast? What does one call it? There seem to be no words for this.

My mother is told she is lucky by her doctors, by the nurses and aids, by a woman at the cancer survivor group, a group to which she will not return. The cancer hasn't spread. Lucky.

She visits with women—friends and friends of friends, this sad sisterhood—who have had mastectomies and reconstructions. They lead her into their bedrooms, unbutton their blouses or lift their shirts, turn slowly to show her their new breasts. There should be gifts given and received here: silken garments; rich, fragrant soups; colorful stones smoothed by the sea; and poems—but not about spring or verdant valleys, nothing budding.

VI.

My friend calls ahead because he knows some people have issues with Barbie. He pronounces "issues" carefully, accenting the second syllable for effect. At nine, his daughter has decided she has outgrown Barbie. "Are you sure it's okay?" he asks.

"Bring her on," I say, because I know the thing denied becomes the thing most coveted. And already my girl has lingered in the Barbie aisle, has looked with longing and hunger at the array of Barbies in their sparkling gowns. I can handle Barbie, I think, Barbie of the tiny feet and waist, the pink pink lips, the wide eyes, pert nose, and breasts—those stunning, nippleless domes.

I was expecting a couple of Barbies—maybe a Ken thrown in for good measure, a few scrappy outfits—but my friend and his daughter arrive with a big plastic bin. It is filled with Barbies, fifteen or more, in all sorts of elaborate costumes. There is a mermaid Barbie with a jeweled bikini top, a bride Barbie, a flamenco Barbie in red and gold ruffles, a cyclist Barbie with a hot pink helmet, a geisha Barbie in a kimono. The Barbies are blond, brunette, redheaded. Their skin is pink, coffee-colored, chocolate, but they look remarkably the same. The lone Ken doll has gold stars in his painted-on hair.

"Thank you," I say. My girl is nearly shaking with delight. I want to say "What a windfall," but I can't find the word in all the excitement. All that comes to me is "landfill," and I know that's the wrong word. "Thank you," I say again.

What is it with Barbie? As soon as you know it, she's stripped down, naked and sprawled out, her party frocks and nylons turned inside out in the rush. She's shameless. We will spend the next few years stepping over naked Barbies, and her tiny accessories—sparkly high-heeled shoes and opera gloves, fur-lined coats. Her breasts, erased of nipples, are purely decorative, just another accessory one can acquire: "We can go to the mall with Skipper," says one of the Barbies when a button is pushed on her back.

Occasionally I worry about Barbie's bad influence. Certainly I don't want my girl to loathe her body, to become anorexic or bulimic, to turn promiscuous or materialistic, to feel heterosexuality is compulsory.

"You know, don't you, that no one really looks like this," I say. I'm helping her groom the Barbies, their long hair dreadlocky from extensive play.

"I know," she says.

I push on. "Real breasts aren't this big or hard."

"No," my girl says, "breasts are soft pillows."

VII.

She is on the cusp, my girl. Gone are the rolls of fat at her thighs, fat made from my milk; gone are the dimpled knuckles, the round toddler belly. At seven, she is lithe and slim, as lovely as a tulip. Sometimes even now, she'll pull at my shirt, tuck herself up there. "Nursy?" she says, part joke, part test.

"Soon you'll have breasts of your own," I say, though it seems impossible.

One night, I come across her in the bathtub pulling at her chest.

"What are you doing?" I ask, squatting by the side of the tub.

"Seeing what I'll look like when I get breasts," she says grinning.

"Are you looking forward to that?" I ask. The air is steamy around us.

She releases her chest and splashes back. Water sloshes over the side of the tub. "I can hardly wait!"

I don't tell her now that it hurts at first, though I remember vividly that nugget of tenderness at each nipple, and my confusion and fear—was I dying? That can all come later. Now I only smile and hold out the towel for her, my girl.

The World's Most
Beautiful Baby—Take Two

JOYCE
MAYNARD

My daughter Audrey—my first baby, born just after my twenty-fourth birthday—was a beauty from the start. She emerged from my body with a full shock of black hair and large eyes, black as coffee beans, and skin of a shade that could leave a person with the impression that she'd spent the winter in someplace like Cabo San Lucas or Palm Beach instead of my belly. What I felt, looking down at her as she lay in my arms that first day, and the many that followed, was the deepest kind of love—and something else: the deepest kind of pride. I had made this person. She was mine. And the fact that she was also beautiful reflected, surely, on me.

People told me babies' hair always fell out. She'd end up bald as an egg, they said, but I didn't believe it, and I was right. At an age when other babies—the ones in the doctor's waiting room ready for their neonatal visits—remained shriveled and bald, Audrey didn't just have hair, she had a hairdo. Her lashes were so long they cast shadows on her cheeks. Her mouth was a rosebud. "You should send her picture somewhere," people told me. "She could have her face on the Pampers box." In Latin America, maybe.

I didn't pursue a modeling career for my daughter, but secretly, I loved it that I had not simply a healthy, wonderful, cuddly, perfect baby girl, but a beautiful one. In years past, I had sometimes felt irritation with my own mother at the way she seemed to appropriate what she perceived as my successes in life as her own. The way, when I got anorectically thin at the end of high school and beyond, she—as a lifelong dieter—seemed to delight in my size-2 body. The way she instructed me in what to wear for trips to visit my grandparents, how she pressed me for details of what went on after the prom with my high-school boyfriend. It all contributed to a feeling that she had lost sight of where her identity ended and mine began.

Once I became a mother myself, though, a glimmer of understanding came to me. I remember a day, a few weeks after Audrey's birth, when her father and I were headed over to the house of friends for a visit. I had spent an hour bathing and dressing Audrey, changing her outfit, deciding which of the many dresses I'd been given—newborn size 0; they'd fit her for about two weeks—to put on her that day. Finally I'd made my selection, brushed her hair, inserted her shell toes in their booties, and headed out to the car, ready for the visit—except for the fact that I had nothing on but my underwear. Where once I would have primped a fair amount myself for an outing like this, now the only beauty I considered was that of my daughter. For nine months, I'd given over my body to her. Now she had my brain, and something else besides: my vanity. I no longer sought to be the fairest in the land. Only the mother of the fairest.

When your daughter is an infant, you can do what you will with her, of course. Hairdo selections, outfits, shoes: She's like the best doll you ever had. Her entry into your life is likely to herald one of your least glamorous and attractive moments (belly stretched out, waist thickened, hair lank, circles under the eyes), and maybe that fact all the more encourages the impulse to avoid thoughts of your own appearance and turn instead (obsessively, perhaps) to those of your child.

Later, you come to love so many things about your child: her sense of humor, her sweetness, her love of animals, the way she dances, the way she smiles at other babies, or the joy she takes in a ball, a rubber spatula, a bubble. But a newborn, if she isn't precisely a blank slate, still remains far less well known, even to her own parents, than she will be one day. What you do know is her face. Her body. The sound of her voice, crying or cooing. Not surprisingly, you come to love those things about her.

When Audrey was about six months old, I wrote an article for Family Circle about the pride and vanity a mother feels over the physical appearance of her child. The piece was called "How It Feels to Be the Mother of the World's Cutest Baby," and to illustrate it, the magazine requested that I bring Audrey to New York for a photo shoot.

I dressed her in the most elaborate of her many dresses for the occasion. The photographer and I propped her up on a throne of pillows, bathed in light, while a stylist fluffed her amazing black hair. "Are those eyelashes real?" he asked me.

The story I'd written was meant to be humorous, of course. I didn't really believe my daughter, or anyone's daughter for that matter, could lay claim to being the cutest baby in the world, but the fact that I and my fellow mothers tended to view our children that way was a phenomenon worthy of note, and of a certain wry self-deprecation. *Look at what's* happened to me, I was saying. Six months ago I had a baby, and it turned me into a crazy person.

Not the only one, however. When the magazine hit the stands, I was deluged with letters, and so were the editors of *Family Circle*. How dare this woman say her baby was the cutest, the authors of these letters wrote (deadly serious, all of them), when in fact that distinction happened to belong to their own baby girl? (Photograph enclosed.)

When Audrey was not quite two years old, she contracted the chicken pox. She itched all over, of course, but the challenge came when scabs formed on her scalp, and despite my vigilance, she scratched one off, just on the crown of her head. The spot left where the scab had been was probably no more than an eighth of an inch in circumference, but I actually wept, thinking of my beautiful daughter with a bald spot. I called my best friend, Laurie, to talk about it and found her immersed in a sorrow of her own. "Leah chipped a tooth yesterday," she said, speaking of her own baby girl.

"At least it was a baby tooth," I said. Still, if you'd heard the two of us that day, you might have thought our children had lost limbs instead of a microscopic piece of tooth, a few hair follicles. The way some men are about the first scratch in a new car was how I was about that microscopic bald spot. My beautiful daughter was no longer perfect.

As Audrey grew, her exotic, otherworldly beauty blossomed—and I admit, so did the joy and misplaced pride of ownership I took in it. I sewed buttons in the shapes of ducks and kittens on her dresses and stitched appliqués of flowers on her overalls. Her thick hair grew to her waist, and though it required hours of brushing, I didn't mind. When she was six, she came home from school with a note: "Audrey has lice." I put a video of *Gone with the Wind* in the VCR, and from the time Scarlett O'Hara first got laced into her bodice to the moment Clark Gable carried her up the staircase, I picked those lice eggs out of Audrey's waist-length hair, uncomplaining. The alternative—cutting her hair—was just too painful to contemplate, and not just for my daughter. For her mother, most of all.

But here's what happened. Not all at once, but gradually: My daughter ceased to let me turn her into my dress-up doll. She picked out her own dresses, and sometimes the choices were very far from ones I'd make. She put together combinations that were her idea of fashion, not mine. She didn't like to brush her hair, but she didn't like me brushing it either. As a result, she sometimes went off to school looking like a mess.

I hated it that I cared as much as I did. Sometimes we argued, sometimes bitterly, over what she wore or over the tangles in her hair. Really though, the source of our battles went deeper. My daughter was separating from me.

For a while—around the time her father and I divorced, when she was eleven and twelve—she got chubby. Then she got a haircut that turned out badly, and for months she wore a pink velvet hat on her unflattering bubble cut. I knew—having had a mother who cared too much about my weight when I was young—that I had to stay out of this one, but sometimes, watching her scoop handfuls of cookie dough from the bowl, it was all I could do not to speak of the calorie count. She would sit at the counter, eating Häagen-Dazs straight out of the carton. More than once I got a spoon and joined her just so she wouldn't eat the whole thing herself. I cared about my weight, too. But I would rather consume the extra calories myself than see them go to my daughter.

These are dirty little secrets I'm confessing here. It might be easier to admit that I got drunk around my child, or yelled at her, or neglected to attend her junior high band concert; easier to say (though it's not true) that I was this vain about my own looks, this self-absorbed with my own hair and clothes and body, than to say that I loved that my daughter was beautiful, that I took inordinate pleasure in how she looked. But the truth is, I did.

Her face wasn't the only thing I loved about her. Not even what I loved best. There was so much to love: her smile, her laugh. Her capacity to make friends wherever she went. Her tenderness to her little brothers. Her quick mind. Her boundless zest for life. Still, when I traveled away from home, I derived huge pleasure from taking her photograph out of my wallet and showing it to people, and hearing them say "My god, she's beautiful."

Here is the worst shame for me: That when my daughter wasn't beautiful—and sometimes she wasn't—I grieved the loss of her beauty more than I grieved the appearance of lines on my own face, or my graying hair, or the fact that my legs were no longer as slim as they once had been. One day I looked at my daughter—my dark, exotic beauty, a girl who inherited from her Eastern European grandmother not only thick dark hair and dark skin and dark eyes, but also, I realized, a faint fuzz of dark hair on her upper lip. And what I felt was a shiver of regret and a terrible absence of the old familiar pride.

Audrey was thirteen then, and kids at school had teased her a few times that she had a moustache. I might have told her, "So did Frida Kahlo, and she was one of the great beauties of the world." I might have said, "Those kids don't sound like the kind of people to be friends with." I might have put my arms around her and said, "To me, you are perfect."

Instead what I told her was, "You know, we could go to an electrolysist and take care of that."

How could I do that to the girl I loved more than any other on the planet? I was a girl once myself—a girl who once thought her eyebrows were too thick and plucked them obsessively, a girl who slept with Saran Wrap around her waist to lose inches from her middle, a girl who lived on one container of boysenberry yogurt per day for an entire summer when she was seventeen. I was a girl whose own mother had been thrilled as I dwindled to ninety-seven pounds, without a clue that what it took to get there was my putting my index finger down my throat every day.

I was a woman (the very same woman who breastfed this very daughter and the two sons that followed) who at age thirty-five wrote a check to a plastic surgeon for $3,000 for the insertion (through her armpits) of silicone implants, because the boyfriend she'd met, after her divorce, had suggested it might be a good idea if she did something so her breasts weren't so droopy. I was a woman who did one hundred sit-ups a night in the dark. I was a woman who at the age of forty had a dentist fill in the gap between her front teeth (that she actually sort of liked) because she recognized that most women didn't have a gap like that, and she wanted to look more like everybody else. I was a woman who sometimes, in bed at night, put a hand on her belly—no longer flat, after giving birth three times—and, instead of registering appreciation for what it had borne and acceptance for its forgivable softness, felt instead a small sensation of regret and disgust.

I was a woman who should have known as well as anyone the pain that women go through trying to replicate a certain accepted image of female beauty and present it to the world. And in spite of knowing the cost of living that way, I was ready to see my treasured only daughter experience the same kind of pain I had gone through—and the same inevitable disappointment at falling short of the ideal.

I think I know the real kind of pain I wanted to spare Audrey. I wanted my daughter to be spared the humiliation of rejection; the loneliness of feeling unworthy, unloved, unnoticed. And I actually supposed the way a woman best protected herself against those things was to make sure she was pretty enough—beautiful enough, if possible—that she would hold power over those who might otherwise hurt and reject her.

But Audrey, to her credit, wasn't buying that idea. I would prefer to say that I had recognized, for myself, the lack of wisdom in trying to maintain power in a cruel world by accepting the world's cruel rules, but I think Audrey decided on her own—not all at once of course, but gradually, over the years of her teens and the years that have followed—to live by some other code than the one that would have placed her where so many of us end up: on a lifelong mission to look like someone else's concept of a beautiful woman. Somewhere along the line, my daughter decided that she would love herself the way she was. And of course, that has made her more powerful than conventional beauty (which always fades) ever could have.

I wish I could say I simply and purely celebrated her choices to give up shaving her legs, to discontinue the electrolysis on her lip, to let her belly—no longer chubby, but round in the way a woman's belly is meant to be—show over the top of her jeans without feeling a need to tell her to hold in her stomach, as I have spent the last thirty years doing. At times, I tried to suggest small concessions: Why not wear a bra at least, to protect against the future effects of gravity? (In the end, she did.) I told her I'd pay for contact lenses to replace her glasses. (No thanks.) I took her to a department store to buy fashionable tops to replace the pillowcases with armholes cut in the sides that she chose to wear for a while. She ended up with a pair of running shoes instead.

But while I imagined I was teaching my daughter how to look like a more attractive woman, she taught me, instead, the nature of true female beauty. It is a glow that radiates from her, and a person doesn't need to be an impossibly biased mother to spot it when she dances into a room.

When she was nineteen, Audrey shared a dormitory suite with five other young women at UC Santa Cruz. I remember the first time I paid her a visit there, sometime in the fall of that year. I walked into the common room the six young women shared and saw on the wall a row of life-sized plaster molds of six naked female torsos. No faces—the girls had cast their bodies from the neck to the waist, painted them silver, and mounted them over the couch.

These were young women—women who had yet to nurse babies or celebrate their fortieth, thirtieth, or even twentieth birthdays—and still there was not a single pair of what someone in Hollywood might term "perfect breasts" displayed on that wall.

Still, they were beautiful. More so, in fact, because they were not perfect. And because they were real. The same thing can be said about my daughter.

I once thought I was the one who created her. I suppose I thought, back when my daughter was little, that she would be a reflection of me. But I was wrong about that, as is every mother who supposes her child belongs to her. In the twenty-eight years since I gave birth to Audrey, I have learned that my daughter created her own self, and that while she was at it, she helped make me who I am too. She is not a reflection of me. If she reflects anything, it's the light of the sun.

She wears her hair in a long braid down her back now. Except for a little lipstick now and then, she wears no makeup. She moves like a woman who knows how to dance *bachata* and *merengue,* which she does. Some people think she's Cuban, but mostly they just ask where in the world she comes from, because truthfully, she looks like nobody but her own self. Not her father. Not any of her grandparents. Not her brothers. Certainly not me. She is her own creation, her own work of art.

Baby Fat

CATHERINE NEWMAN

Zipped into a too-small stretchy sleeper, with her scribble of dark hair and lopsided grin, our baby daughter was a wide-bellied Elvis impersonator. Naked, she was all origami marshmallow: sweet flesh folded into a puffy configuration of limbs and tummy. It was impossible not to nibble her dinner-roll feet, her—pass the mustard!—cocktail-frank fingers. Oh, the luscious Santa Rosa plums of her cheeks! And if your house keys went missing, well, did you think to check underneath the many soft tiers of her chin? You never knew what you might find in there.

In short, she was a gorgeous baby—a fact that was grasped fully by her many admirers. "Ooooh," a friend pretend-fretted over her dimpled calves, "this is the worst case of *chubbylegitis* I've ever seen." Another marveled that, with her dark, glittering eyes, she looked like Audrey Hepburn, "But, you know, *fat*." We called her "Fattykins." We called her "Chubbalubs." We called her "the sea lion pup" and kissed her all over and went dotty with love.

Which made other people's concern about her all the more mystifying. "He's a robust little thing, isn't he?" a bank teller once praised, and when I said, "I know! She's so sturdy!" this person unsmiled her mouth, wrinkled up her nose and said, "Oh. It's a girl." Our son had also been fat as a milk-fed pumpkin, and his broad, grinning face had invited nothing but delight. But with our daughter—well, people seemed inclined to worry. Or, even with no worry in sight, to reassure. "I'm sure she'll slim down by summertime," a stranger offered in the frozen foods aisle. The baby was two months old then, sleeping across my chest in a front pack. "Thank God!" I said. "Because there's this really hot bikini we want her to wear? And she'll never fit into it like this."

"She'll grow out of it." "They thin out by the time they're walking." "Maybe you should offer her water instead." There was no shortage of comfort or advice. This shouldn't have surprised me, of course. It's not exactly a secret that our culture still likes its women—and, as it turns out, its female infants—thin. It doesn't take a course called "Misogyny and the Media" to familiarize yourself with this phenomenon: simply pick up a magazine, look at a billboard, notice a diet food item, watch a movie, turn on the TV, or shop at a clothing store. Or just grab your own belly with two hands—like a stretch-marked, ham and cheese submarine sandwich—and experience the fat pangs of self-loathing.

Indeed. Here's where things get complicated. Because while the baby's amplitude invoked only my doting admiration, my own—those fleshy curtains hanging from my arms and back, for example—felt like the lumpy harbingers of some kind of postpartum apocalypse. I had loved being huge and pregnant—loved the purposeful girth of myself—but now the leftovers, however minor in scale, depressed me. Like the belly! The belly! Ugh. You know focaccia, how the baker presses his fingertips into the dough so that olive oil can pool into all those pale, bready dimples? It was like that. Come summertime, despite my ever-expanding passion for my ever-expanding baby, and despite this same baby's abiding love of my own milky, sustaining body, I stuffed my new torso into the sausage casing of a swimsuit and cringed. My analytical, feminist self and my generous, earthy self both revered the flesh that had created and nourished these beautiful kids; my svelte, stingy superego just thought I was a fattykins—and not in a yummy-baby way.

Sure, you might, think. Who doesn't want to see her own collarbones? Who doesn't want her thighs to stop moving at around the same time as the rest of the body? Who doesn't feel better with a bit of the excess trimmed away? But it's a slippery slope: One minute you're at the top, standing on a chair to look at your own butt in the mirror, the next minute you're sliding down with a Diet Coke in your hand and a bad feeling in your heart. And the stakes of self-esteem—the unconditional kind that loves even the self's big legs—are high. This chunka-munka girl baby who lives in our midst—this now two-year-old who is so amply delicious that a complete stranger grabbed my arm on the beach and said, "Don't you just want to bite her?"—this person is going to need to grow up into a girl, and then a woman, who feels good about herself. And that good feeling is going to have to come from us, from herself. Wise strangers aside, the world is not likely to wash over her in gentle waves of worthiness. We know this already. Instead there will be the nasty flotsam of impossible standards, the greasy black tides of contemptuous appraisal, and a disparaging undertow. She will be too fat or thin, too bosomy or boardlike, too gangly-tall or stumpy. Whatever her anatomical coordinates, they will never be quite right. Or rather, their very rightness is going to have to come from the True North of self-confidence; this will be her only guide in the hazy, befuddling—and, ideally, dazzling—journey of female incarnation.

So my job now is to love myself, because . . . well, not to be immodest, but the baby wants to be just like me—even though it's not from me that she learned to bounce through the house like a happy, round ball yelling for cottage cheese. This person the baby imitates will have to be the one who looks at herself in the mirror and smiles. The person who lets her deranged husband grab her by her big, big legs and feels sexy and pleased. The person who says, "I'd love one!" to another sliver of New York's best cheesecake and who looks happily at ease in the summer beach photos, swimsuit and all. Not the person who watched Jennifer Jason Leigh waste away in the '80s TV bulimia drama *The Best Little Girl in the World*, thought, "She's so thin! Cool!" and then went on to trade strength for slightness, health for appearance, pleasure for control, and a body for an idea. Not the one who looked at herself as if through the eyes of a hateful stranger. Not that person, no matter what.

Bodies are amazing things. If my baby grows up and wants to wear hers as a kind of armor, fine. If she wants to work it in the service of athletics or seduction or reproduction, great. But God help me if she experiences it as an anchor, a shroud, a hair shirt, a glass ceiling, a bull's eye, a pox. Let her always love herself the way she does now. The way she does when she says, in a falsetto imitation of our fond foolishness, "Am I such a gorgeouskins?" Or when she wants to go to bed with no pajamas, and she wraps her arms around her own silky self and cries, "I want to sleep with just my tummy!" Let her always love that tummy.

And let me be more like her.

GARDEN CITY

Me and My Girls

AMY
BLOOM

I'm standing in front of the theater with my mother and my two daughters on a cold winter night. One daughter left the house wearing my pantyhose, my earrings, and my jacket. Now she's also wearing my lipstick and my gloves. I stand in front of my other daughter to block the wind and hand her lip balm, Kleenex, and my scarf. My mother hands me her gloves. We have all made each other who we are.

I became a stepmother at twenty-three and had my daughters at twenty-six and twenty-nine—young only by the standards of the women I knew. My friends all had their babies ten or fifteen years later, while being a mother has framed most of my adult life. A reader of child-development books since I was a teenage baby sitter, I expected to recognize myself in my daughters, and I did. But reading did not prepare me for the enveloping pleasure of that recognition. Even the harsh, uninhibited expressions of anger, dislike, or disdain were not truly disturbing. They were my facial expressions, my hand gestures, my eye rolling, transmitted through these newly beloved, always beautiful features and modified by their distinctly different temperaments, but still part of me.

My older daughter was born three weeks late and has been eager to get to the party ever since. Her buoyancy echoed my own and increased it. Every positive move I made toward her was magnified and returned. We made each other braver, stronger, happier. I wore her as both shield and laurel wreath—gorgeous, charming, smart, verbal to an astonishing degree—and I didn't give a damn what anyone thought about my matted lumpiness and the banana goo on my shoulder. We watched ourselves in each other's eyes and were delighted.

She fell into a November-cold pond on the way home from first grade and came dripping and blue into the after-school center. I put my coat around her and tried to coax the story from her (stories do not have to be coaxed from this girl, who tells them with Southern embellishment and a host of different voices). She shook her head, her lips clamped shut. In the car, out of sight from the other kids, she told me the story and cried. The big kids had been testing the early ice, so she did too. She went too far and slid into the water up to her hips. It was very important to her not to cry, so she just climbed out, shook herself off, and said, with a great effort at fourth-grade sophistication, "My mother will kill me for getting wet," and hauled her soggy, freezing little self up the hill. They did not see her cry. I was so lost in admiration for her guts that it was a few minutes into our cold, wet hug before I yelled at her for being reckless. Then we talked about the word "reckless" and what it might mean to have "reck" in the first place, and I fell a little more in love.

Someone recently asked her what she saw of herself in me. "What don't I see of myself in her?" she said. And I was flattered but not surprised. She has most of my adult skills and several of my foibles. She takes on too much, can't resist giving advice, comforts the world before gauging her own feelings, prizes her competence perhaps too highly. And when I see these things in her, it makes me look at me. I work on me, in large part for her and her sister; I make myself admit to vulnerability and mistakes so that she, in particular, will see that there's no shame in that. I try to live the life I want, because that's what I wish for her. Because of her, I have gone on rollercoaster rides, worn blue frosting (from the Cookie Monster cake) under my fingernails for days on end, listened to three-volume stories of teenage intrigue, gnashed my teeth over unreturned phone calls, rolled and unrolled my jeans cuffs when she told me to, had great fun, and felt my heart come close to breaking. Because of me, she is who she is. Because of her, I am too.

My second daughter was born amidst bright lights and bustling nurses and didn't care for any of it. She squinched up her perfect face and tried to burrow back into the blanket. A few hours later, cautiously and curiously, she opened her eyes. An observer was born.

She reminded me of my childhood self: watchful, thoughtful, easily moved, easily hurt. I wanted to wrap her in the softest, strongest armor and keep everything but puppies, guppies, and rose petals away from her. As smart and funny and beautiful as the first, but in different ways, she has been teaching me about honoring difference ever since her birth.

This is the "shy" child who made her debut in our neighborhood by going door to door, ringing doorbells and not only requesting playmates but describing their ideal characteristics. ("Do you have a little girl? A nice little girl who likes swings? Who shares?") This is my literature-resister who reads Emily Dickinson and Mark Doty; my nonperformer who sang her bat mitzvah prayers with quiet grace and confident smiles. That's the thing—I expected the quiet grace. I didn't quite expect the notes to ring out to the last row; I didn't expect a speech that was forceful and funny, as well as sensible and interesting; I didn't expect her to crack jokes with the rabbi as she moved through a two-hour ceremony in which all eyes were upon her. I should have. She has been trying to show me that waiting is not always passive, that stepping back is not always fear, that she knows best who she is and that I would be wise to follow her lead.

My older daughter and I are skilled strategists; we find the way to go around the rock, to go over the rock; we even occasionally get someone else to move it for us. My younger one splits it open. She cannot take the easy way or even the sensible way, but when she approaches the problem, she is as daring and powerful and sure as a thunderbolt, and she is the only one unsurprised by the sight of two granite pieces teetering gently on the ground.

She apparently began sucking her finger in utero and didn't stop for the next ten years. Once school began, I was filled with the usual hopes, a persistent fear that she would be teased about her finger and, as she entered second, then third, then fourth grade, the small ugly wish that there would be just enough teasing to get her to stop. Amazingly, since she was neither ashamed nor secretive about her habit, she wasn't teased—except by a few adults, who apparently believed that their jokes would break a lifelong habit. Had anyone tried to josh them out of overeating? Nail biting? Overspending? (Never mind. I'm still mad at those people.) The teasing picked up a bit at the beginning of fifth grade, and she said she wanted to stop. We rapidly cycled through the hot pepper nail polish, the reward charts, and the calendars. She sighed and said, "I guess when I'm ready, I'll stop." And she patted my hand reassuringly.

One night, as she was going to bed, she said, "I think I won't suck my finger tonight." I smiled—if it was that easy, surely she would have stopped before. "I think," she said, "I just won't suck my finger anymore." I looked in on her before I went to bed: Her hand was under her pillow.

In the morning, she went through the moderately stressful getting-ready-for-school routine without sucking her finger. When she came home from school, I couldn't help asking, and she told me no, no finger sucking. Did she want to go back to our reward system and pick out a present to reinforce a week of no finger sucking?

"Why? I'm done. It doesn't matter if you get me a present or not, now, Mommy. I'm done." And she was. Forever. The strength of ten and the heart of a lion.

They've learned from each other's strengths and weaknesses and from mine (my weaknesses are, of course, one of their great bonds in frustration as well as amusement). The older one has toughened the other; the younger one demonstrates a nonconforming streak that impresses, and even inspires, the older one. We are loyal; we like dim sum; we don't mix our metals; we don't tolerate prejudice. We share a sense of humor that is all raised eyebrows and storytelling and neither puns nor jokes (we do actually have four jokes between us, two of which are funny). They dress me now, these tall, breathtaking young women, more than I (am allowed to) dress them, and the younger one says, having picked out my shoes, "You're pretty." And the older one says, admiring her handiwork (and rolling her eyes at my choice of necklace), "Yeah, you're cute." And I know that we all are seeing our same pieces refracted and placed differently on three women, all partially dressed in each other's clothes, all held in each other's eyes, and each one created, in part, by the other two.

Girl Talk

SUZANNE
KAMATA

Among my fantasies upon learning that I would be the mother of a girl: We would wear matching dresses, as my own mom and I sometimes did. I would take her to ballet lessons and watch her twirl on the stage. I would teach her to read in English and introduce her to Nancy Drew. We would celebrate Girl's Day, arranging all those beautiful dolls in their bright kimonos together, as is the custom in her native Japan, but she would also be fully exposed to American culture. When she turned twelve, we would take a trip to Paris together, leaving her dad and twin brother behind in Tokushima. And once we got through the prickly days of her adolescence, during which even the way I chewed my food would be uncool, we would sit on the edge of her bed and have long talks about her dreams of being an astronaut or a doctor, about that boy she was in love with. I remembered sitting at the kitchen table with my own mom after school, having the same kinds of conversations. I wanted that with my daughter.

Then Lilia and her brother, Jio, were born fourteen weeks premature. Lilia's brain was injured, and I realized that, due to her cerebral palsy, we wouldn't be going to ballet lessons after all. When I learned at six months that my daughter was deaf, I thought, "We won't be able to engage in girl talk," and I started to mourn.

I had imagined, from the time that I sat next to my babies' Plexiglas isolettes, singing and speaking to them, that we would bond through language. I would share all of my childhood favorite books with them—the adventures of Madeline, Babar, Clifford the Big Red Dog—and I would write stories for them in English. They would grow up bilingual, speaking my language as fluently as their father's Japanese. While their dad still doesn't understand everything I say (and vice versa) even after twelve years of marriage, I would be able to speak my native tongue at normal speed and be perfectly understood. I saw my language as a gift I could give my children.

No matter how much trouble I had with Japanese, I could always turn to English, my refuge. For several years I made my living teaching English conversation to Japanese children and adults. After work, I could pop *Out of Africa* or *Casablanca* into the VCR (the video stores are stocked with American movies). My TV was bilingual, which meant I could push a button to hear American television shows in English. I could read books, magazines, even the *Japan Times* with ease in my native language, and I had native-speaker friends from England, Australia, and the U.S. to talk with.

Lilia, I knew, needed a language of her own, one that she could understand without strain. Even with a hearing aid and a cochlear implant, the spoken word would be a challenge for her. Lip reading is inexact: "bomb" and "mom" look the same. But she could learn sign language.

The idea of learning sign language via Japanese was daunting. To be honest, although I had achieved a degree of proficiency in Japanese, I was tired of struggling along in my second language. I'd studied French in college, when I was a lot younger. I'd read that language acquisition starts to get difficult after the age of fourteen, when the brain's pathways become established. At thirty-four, I couldn't really see myself tackling a fourth language. I'd once tried to teach English to a group of women in their sixties who couldn't remember simple greetings from one week to the next. It was pretty clear that it becomes harder to learn a new language as we age. Still, to impose only English or even Japanese upon Lilia seemed selfish. Like it or not, I would need to learn to sign too.

Lilia's first signed word was "milk"—a thumb tilted toward the mouth. She learned the signs for "ouch" and "dangerous." She quickly acquired the signs for animals—"dog," "cat," "rabbit." Her first sentence, executed in our backyard, was, "Where's the frog?" It would be months before she was able to make the sign for "mother"—index finger brushing the cheek, followed by a fist with the pinky extended.

Meanwhile, I spoke English to Lilia and her brother. She learned to say "up" and "open" and "off"—words that are easy to read on the lips—but her teachers at the deaf school insisted that I use only Japanese, that it would be too difficult for her to learn more than one spoken language at a time.

I didn't believe them. The brain is an amazing thing, after all. I'd read about a deaf girl in New York City who spoke and signed in both the English of her adopted country and the Russian of her immigrant parents. I also knew of a girl who had a Japanese mother and an American father and who was learning both parents' languages.

But Lilia's father worked long hours, and so there was no one at home to reinforce the Japanese she learned at school. And although I spoke English at home with her, I had to speak Japanese when I was in her classroom. I was worried this would confuse her, so I did my best to speak and write in Japanese with Lilia at home, and I continued to study Japanese Sign Language.

I have often thought that my life in Japan until the birth of my children was meant to prepare me for raising my deaf daughter. Like Lilia, I am often frustrated when others don't understand what I'm trying to say. I understand only a percentage of the conversations that go on around me. Sometimes I'm just guessing, imagining.

By default, the one who understands her best is not her twin brother, with whom she shares a birth date and a bedroom; not her father, who like Lilia, is a native of Japan; not her grandmother, who is hard-of-hearing and thus similarly disabled; but her foreign, fish-out-of-water mother. I am the only one in our household, other than Lilia, who is learning JSL.

According to deaf-school policy, mothers must accompany their children to kindergarten. In the days of the early intervention program, back when Lilia was one, two, and three, Jio came along and picked up signs as well. The staff made it clear, however, that her brother wouldn't be welcome further on. They'd tried to mix hearing and deaf children about twenty years ago, they told me, but it didn't work out. While it may be the norm in England, the Tokushima School for the Deaf was finished with integration.

We sent our son to a private three-year preschool, where he would master Japanese and learn to make swords out of rolled up paper. Lilia and I stayed at the deaf school. At home, Jio occasionally called upon me to translate for Lilia. Her dad sometimes muddled along with made-up signs that meant nothing to Lilia unless I stepped in to correct him.

Last year, Lilia started to write on her own. First she learned to write her name and then, without being taught, her brother's name. One day, she handed me a picture she'd drawn of me. She had written "mama" in Japanese next to it. I hugged her long and hard and tacked the picture on my bulletin board, next to my computer.

I am thrilled by the progress she has made, but I also worry that I won't be able to keep up with her. Soon she'll be signing past my level, and with her heightened visual sense, I believe she'll find it easier to learn kanji, the pictograms that make up much of written Japanese, than I have. What if I need a translator to communicate deeply with my own daughter?

My own mother and I both speak English, but it is at times difficult even for us to find common ground. She doesn't understand why I like to sleep with my children, or the attraction of living in a foreign country, or why I vote the way I do. I don't get why she doesn't adore the novels of Barbara Kingsolver. Yet we are bound by blood and love.

At the moment, most of Lilia's formal education is centered on listening and speaking, but at home she fills pages and pages with random Japanese letters. Sometimes I find that she has tried to copy words from some of the many English books we have strewn around the house. She pulls my novels from the bookshelves and lugs them around in her Pooh backpack. She still says "open" and "off." I'm starting to have faith that one way or another, we will find the words we need to say what we have to say to each other.

Last week she turned six, and this is how we talk: She sees that I am wearing my pink polo dress, and she signs that she wants to wear her new twirly pink dress. She points to a picture of Daichi, a sweet, big-eyed boy in her class, and kisses it. She uses her language to tell me that she's the doctor and I'm the patient and I'd better lie down on the sofa so that she can give me a shot. I understand what she's saying, and I obey.

Daughter Dread

**VICKY
MLYNIEC**

When I was pregnant and people asked, "Do you want a boy or a girl?" the answer "Boy!" burst from my lips with such conviction that it startled me. No high-tech tests had revealed the baby's sex, but even with the boy–girl odds being fifty-fifty, no girls' names on my list ever got circled. We roared off to the hospital with a boy's name long settled and a big blank for the girl. "What'll we do if it's a girl?" my husband asked. I shrugged, not planning to have one.

Deep down, I assumed I'd fall in love with the baby, boy or girl, as soon as it was placed in my arms. But the strength of my preference worried me. Why this daughter dread? Was I a traitor to my sex for so clearly preferring boys? Was my girl-baby phobia some convoluted self-esteem problem, some deep-seated sexism I wasn't aware of? My best guess was that I didn't want to deal with the staggering emotional complexity of raising a daughter. Having a daughter would mean adding to the already huge responsibility of child-rearing the task of untangling my past from my daughter's present.

Raising a daughter might seem easier with so many common interests to share. After all, I'd been a little girl myself, though reportedly an odd one. I never wanted to dig through my mother's jewelry box or clomp around in her high heels. I was mystified by dolls and why brushing their stiff hair with tiny brushes or tucking them into bed was supposed to be fun. Suddenly I faced the prospect of having a daughter who, in a few short years, might want to try on makeup I didn't have and drag me down the pink aisle in the toy store, pleading with me to buy little homemaker play sets and dolls with more changes of clothes than Britney.

"Stereotype!" I chided myself as these images paraded through my mind. I knew full well the activities I shunned are things girls have every right to do. In fact, it's a normal stage in gender development for a girl to try on various female roles in order to forge her own identity. According to all witnesses, I missed this stage.

"Don't worry," friends told me, "Your daughter might be just like you." But why should she be? I didn't want to mold my child into a mini-me. But could I be as reasonable as my friend Suzi? When I raised my eyebrows at her five-year-old daughter, who was decked out in frills, lace, patent leather shoes, and purse to match, Suzi countered, "She's allowed to be a girl, you know." If I had a daughter, could I get out of her way? Could I let her be the girl, the person, she wanted to be? Could I hide my disinterest in—at times distaste for—girlish things? Surely she'd sniff out my disapproval like a bloodhound, and my phony interest in French braiding and making sequined T-shirts would mess her up big time.

Having a boy would just be so much easier, I thought. I'd have to deal with, at worst, a lot of boyish energy, maybe some lack of sensitivity to feelings, maybe more grunting than communicating. These were things I thought I could work with. At least I'd have a fresh start, a clean slate. Even though I'd never been a boy, I felt I understood boys better than my own sex.

A friend mentioned that women are sometimes jealous of the attention their husbands pay to daughters, that competition can even develop. There was a breath of something valid there, but it had nothing to do with the female vs. female, he's-paying-more-attention-to-her-than-to-me kind of jealousy that my friend meant. I had no doubts about my husband's devotion to me, and I knew he would be a stellar father to a son or daughter. Yet something about the prospect of his being a wonderful father to a daughter disturbed me in a way I couldn't pinpoint. My husband seemed such an innocent in all this. I envied his equanimity, his happiness at the prospect of boy or girl. So simple for him, I thought.

Happily for all, I had a boy. And another. They are noisy and boisterous. They wrestle and whoop, they crash around, and dad gleefully joins in. Nor are they monosyllabic grunters. My female need to communicate and my emotional awareness have produced two sons who just won't shut up.

As I found myself sitting on the floor with my boys, feigning interest in their various passions—hopping little action figures around or driving cars off the edge of the coffee table, again and again—I realized that I probably could just as easily taken on the doll thing. What, after all, was the big deal?

It was watching my husband's easy relationship with his sons, seeing them joke and romp and clump together on the couch, that helped me find the true root of my daughter anxiety. I'd been right about a mother's past merging with a daughter's present, and my friend had been right about a daughter inspiring jealousy in me, but in a way I hadn't suspected.

To see a little girl scooped into my husband's arms, to watch her trail adoringly after him, to see the two walk hand in hand would have made me wish I could have been such a little girl, that I could have had such a comfortable, cozy relationship with my own father. I would have felt with fresh sorrow the awkwardness and distance I always felt with my dad, who loved me but was never at ease with me, who was proud of me but never delighted in me.

Like travel, having children is broadening—only you rarely manage to leave home. Through your children, you relive your childhood, reexamine past relationships, and reach new understandings. My sons have taught me a great deal about myself, but a daughter would have taught me things my sons can't—to understand and appreciate more fully the wonders and complexities of my own gender. The little girl in my mind's eye has already given me something of incalculable value. She helped me see my father with greater compassion by showing me how hard it can be to understand the intricate emotions involved in parent–child relationships. If we pay attention, there's much to be learned from all our children, even from the ones we don't have.

Spilled Wine

JENNIFER
MARGULIS

"**Y**ou ready to order?"

Our waitress had split ends, bangs that needed trimming, and a defeated look on her face. Her white shirt was tucked haphazardly into her black pants, and her apron strings were unevenly tied.

"A martini with extra olives," my father-in-law shouted, taking out his reading glasses to look at the menu, "and a glass of your house wine for my son over here." He gestured proudly to my husband. The girls begged for raspberry lemonade while the baby fidgeted and roared on my lap. Hesperus, five years old, and Athena, three and a half, went to gather books and toys. They came back to their seats just as the drinks arrived.

"The house wine," muttered the waitress, lifting the glass off the tray.

All of a sudden, the full glass slipped out of the waitress's hands, spilling wine all over Athena and shattering on the chair. Athena was completely soaked. She had wine in her hair, in her eyes, on her face, and down her shirt. Athena's whole body shook as she wailed loud enough to arrest every conversation in the restaurant.

"I'm cold, I'm cold," she sobbed, tears streaming from her gray-blue eyes. "I'm all wet! Mommy, Mommy, Mommy! I'm all wet!"

Athena stood trembling as I toweled her off with napkin after napkin. This time, unlike the long months after she was born, her piercing screams subsided quickly.

So quiet in utero that I spent long nights worrying she was really all right, Athena, my second daughter, came into the world calmly enough. Then, as the midwives toweled her off and laid her on my chest, she opened her eyes wide. She took one look around and started screaming—a shrill, piercing sound that made my heart pound with worry. She didn't stop crying for nine months.

When I was still pregnant with Athena, two days past my due date, I received a phone call from the chair of the English Department of the women's college where I worked as a visiting assistant professor.

"Had the baby yet?" he asked curtly. There was no trace of kindness or interest in his question.

"No," my voice was falsely cheerful. "We're still waiting."

When I'd first told the department chair I was pregnant, he had acted totally indifferent to the news. "No problem," he'd said, one eye on his computer screen as he spoke. "We can have someone cover your classes for a week. Besides," he added, "you live so close to campus, it will be easy."

I had gone back to work six weeks after my first daughter, Hesperus, was born. I was unhappy being away from her. The pumping hurt my breasts, I got my first speeding ticket rushing home to feed her between classes, and I missed her so much it was hard not to cry in front of my students. This time, with Athena on the way, I would be mothering a newborn and a toddler. The department chair's oh-so-tempting offer of an entire week off notwithstanding, I wondered if I had a choice about the way I handled my return to work. I went to the chair's supervisor, the dean. He offered me a different option: a semester of maternity leave at half pay. I had no idea at the time that I would be the only faculty member in fifteen years to take advantage of the college's generous policies. I had no idea that my decision would cost me my job, my house, and my livelihood.

"The faculty met two weeks ago," the department chair told me on the phone that day, just before Athena was born. "We won't be able to offer you a job for next year. I'm sorry it had to turn out this way."

We were living in faculty housing. My husband was a stay-at-home dad. I was two days overdue with our second baby, and suddenly we were faced with the possibility of having two children, no job, no place to live, and no idea what we would do. That night I couldn't sleep. The next morning I went into labor.

No wonder Athena protested with shrieking cries a moment after she was born. Keenly intuitive and empathetic, my second daughter already knew that the watery world of her gestation was a lot safer than life outside the womb.

I had always wanted a daughter. The summer I turned thirteen and my mother dropped me off at the Centre écologique in Port-au-Saumon, Canada (and spent more time talking to the janitor than saying goodbye to me), I made a list of all the things I would not do to my own daughter if I ever had one. I wouldn't ignore her. I wouldn't make her feel like a stranger was more important than she was. I would listen when she talked to me. I wouldn't be busy and distracted by work all the time. I would give her a sister so she would not grow up as the only girl in the family. Later I imagined teaching my daughter to be confident and to stand up for herself, not to feel compelled to use her body—as I had—to gain approval from men. And I hoped that she would not come at life like I did as a teenager and young adult—an open wound stung by even the slightest touch.

But when the time came that I was actually pregnant, I worried about how I would relate to a girl child. Growing up with three brothers, a doting father, and an absent mother, I really didn't know anything about girls. But I was so sure that I was having a girl, even though we never found out definitively, that I told my husband I'd eat my hospital gown if the baby were a boy. In the end, my firstborn—a daughter, just as I'd suspected— quelled my fears. Hesperus, a quiet baby who made an ut-ut-ut-ut sound when she wanted to nurse and who barely ever cried, was as easy to love as chocolate cake.

When Athena was born nineteen months after Hesperus and the day after I lost my job, I was so worried about the future, and about taking attention away from my toddler, that I could barely concentrate on my new baby.

It didn't help that Athena was a very fussy newborn. She needed to be held and walked, outside, all the time. Worse, her crying was so shrill and urgent that it scared me and wore away at my already frayed nerves. It was so hard for me to love Athena that I felt miserable almost all the time. I was the worst kind of person, a mother who couldn't love her baby.

One night she woke up, wailing to nurse. It was dark in the room, and I couldn't see well enough to get my breast in her tiny mouth. I tried to switch on the nightlight, but I couldn't find that either. Afraid her crying would awaken Hesperus, I became frantic and furious, pounding the floor with my hand, ostensibly trying to find the nightlight. Athena shrieked louder, and James woke up with a start.

"What's wrong?" He sounded angry.

"I can't nurse her! I can't see. I can't do this," I cried.

"Jennifer," he said, once the light was on and Athena was nursing in peace, "you made so much noise, you scared her."

As I lay there burning with shame and anger, I remembered one of those inane pregnancy videos from the birthing class James and I attended before Hesperus was born. A mother, with her two happy children playing at her feet, told the camera that she was worried that she wouldn't have enough love for two children. "As soon as he was born," she said, smiling at her baby, "I realized I was feeling insecure for nothing. I have so much love in my heart for both of them."

Unlike that woman, when I looked in my heart, I saw nothing but empty space. I was, perhaps, more like my mother than I wanted to be.

"Want to go home?" I asked Athena as she sat, shirtless, in my lap in the restaurant. But Athena shook her head and sighed into my shoulder, her sobs turning into hiccups. A different waitress appeared.

"I brought you something," she said, holding up a white child's T-shirt with the name and logo of the restaurant on it. Athena smiled at her gratefully and touched the lettering.

"What does she have? I want one!" Hesperus came rushing over, nearly upsetting a water glass in her wake. My father-in-law caught it theatrically.

"Thank you," Athena said politely as the waitress helped her with the shirt. She was totally calm now, having fully recovered from the mishap with grace and poise I hadn't expected. Somewhere between the rocky year after she was born and today, my daughter had morphed into a cheerful, self-sufficient, and easygoing little being who could smile moments after having a large glass of wine spilled all over her.

"C'mere, Hesperus," my father-in-law gestured, holding his martini above my older daughter's head. "Tell ya what. I spill this on you and you get a T-shirt too. Deal?"

Athena ate her french fries with an exaggerated smacking of the lips. The dried wine made fruity-smelling dreadlocks out of her straight hair and short bangs. She knew we had all been worried, and she enjoyed making a show of being better. Hesperus's vociferous jealousy over the T-shirt helped too. Our disheveled waitress squatted down to talk to Athena.

"I'm really sorry about what happened," she said. "Sure you're okay?"

"I'm okay," Athena answered her, a little shyly. "You don't have to be sorry anymore." The waitress looked relieved. Athena really meant it: She was no longer feeling bad about the incident, and she didn't want anyone else to feel bad either.

Two more waitresses came to our table. Athena's wine-drenched shirt was in a plastic bag tied at the top. They had been soaking it in salt so it wouldn't stain. Our waitress tore off the check and smiled at Athena.

"Thanks," she whispered to her, "for taking it all so well."

"Thank you," Athena murmured back. The waitress stood up straighter, tucked in her shirt, and smiled a perkier smile at us.

After Athena was born, we moved into a red farmhouse with a big backyard, and James got a job as a lexicographer for Merriam Webster's Dictionary. As our life settled down and the terrible stress of not knowing where to go subsided, things got a little easier with Athena. She learned to talk early on, and she started using words instead of shrieks (most of the time) to tell us what she needed. Although her toddler needs were sometimes still as urgent as those of her babyhood, she could focus for long stretches of time on drawing, trying to put on her pants by herself, or following her sister around the house, pudgy belly hanging over a battered pink tutu. At eighteen months, she decided she had had enough of diapers and started using the potty. Instead of testing me like her older sister had as a toddler, when Athena sensed that I was getting frustrated with her, she'd capitulate: "Okay, Mommy, I cooperate," she'd say. When she did get really upset, I would hold her and hug her and then ask her, "Can I just talk to you for one minute?" and she would nod, quiet down to listen, and look up at me with her gorgeous gray eyes.

Soon I was no longer just going through the motions of caring for my daughter, I was actually feeling the love I had worried would never come. Because that earlier time had been so difficult, and because I felt so guilty about being distracted by work concerns and finding a new home in the weeks after she was born, I think I may have even loved Athena more, to compensate, when we were finally on the other side of it. I still worried that my girls might be having an imperfect childhood with an imperfect mother to care for them, but I realized their experience would not be an exact replay of my own. Athena had taught me that she was her own person and that I needed to love her on her own terms, a lesson I wish my mother had been able to learn with me.

But now we were safely past that rocky start, the hardest part. My girls each had a sister, and I had the daughters I had spent my whole life longing for.

A few months after the wine incident, we were driving back from blueberry picking and planning Hesperus's birthday.

"And I want to go out to eat," Hesperus said.

"Me too!" said Athena.

"But it's not your birthday," Hesperus pointed out.

"On my birthday I want to go out to eat, too," Athena said.

"Where do you want to go?" I asked her.

"To that place, Mommy."

"Which place?"

"You know, the place I got the shower?"

Hesperus and Athena both started giggling, swinging their legs as they laughed.

"The shower?"

"The place where they spilled wine on me, Mommy. It was like a shower! I want to go back there."

I looked back at my girls as their laughter filled the car.

It's true that Athena still cries shrilly and urgently when she's upset, in a way that brings back memories of our stumbling start together. But she's also a girl who can now laugh at mishap and forgive people their shortcomings. The daughter I feared would be too difficult for me to ever enjoy has shown me her true self: a girl with compassion, grace, and a good sense of humor.

As they laughed, I remembered the day of the "shower." To make up for the mishap, the waitress had brought my husband a glass of their finest red, and I tried some. The wine was dry, almost spicy, with hardly any sweetness. It was bitter, foreign, challenging to me, but I took a second sip. I remember noticing that the more I drank it, the more its complex elegance revealed itself to me. I liked it so much, I ordered a second glass for myself.

Garden City

JESSICA BERGER GROSS

While I was pregnant, those few short weeks, I missed my mother, longed for her. I remembered what it was like to be little, sitting next to her on the couch facing the television; her long, neatly kept nails shaped in half-moon ovals; the smooth pads of her fingertips; her fingers, blunt and soft, scratching my skin like she was a cat and I was her post.

My mother still lives in the house where I was raised, on Park Lane in Rockville Centre, a suburb of New York City. The kitchen is different now: the countertops the requisite granite, the appliances stainless steel, a new red plaid couch in front of the television. My father is still there too. That's why I don't go back. My mother has chosen to stay, despite everything that's happened.

I haven't spoken to my mother in almost five years. I didn't invite her to my wedding or to come see the small apartment we recently bought in Cambridge, Massachusetts. I didn't call her when my first book deal came through. She's met my husband, Neil, but just once, years ago. When I was pregnant though, I suddenly worried that maybe it was wrong to keep a child from her own grandmother, and vice versa. The hormones must have made me sentimental, weepy for a mother I never had.

The details are unpleasant, nothing I like talking about. My father couldn't control his temper, and when the rage swelled and pressed against his chest, he let it spill out. The ugly words and name-calling and the physical violence erupted every week or two, flooding through our otherwise normal-enough lives. We were all affected, all victims—my two older brothers, stoic as they were in the face of it, and my mother too—when things were at their worst. But most often me. I was targeted because I was youngest, because I was the only girl, because of nothing. Too sensitive, my mother said. A difficult child, my father agreed. My parents—liberals, educators, with a PhD and a master's degree between them—should have known better. Known to get help, known when to leave. But my mother stayed—after the first time, when I was two and a half, after the next time, and then all the times after that.

My mother stayed because she was afraid to leave. She worked full-time, made a decent salary, but didn't know how to write a check, pay a bill, or fix things around the house when they broke down or fell apart. These things terrified her. Besides, she felt it was important to keep the family together.

Once, after the damage had long been done, when I was all grown up, my mother said that maybe, just maybe, she would leave him after all, but only if I'd promise to take her in, to take care of her as she aged, to be her companion. I didn't want to. I was twenty-eight, just done with graduate school, and looking for a job and an apartment in New York City. I didn't want her for a roommate. So I said no, this was not my responsibility. "I wash my hands of it," I said, and so she stayed. I don't think he hits her anymore. I was the one who really made him mad.

My mother liked taking me clothes shopping. The boys, my two older brothers, stayed home alone or with my father doing boy things: working on the yard, prepping their Sunday newspaper routes, or washing or repairing one of the two family cars. She and I took our outings on Saturday afternoons. There were many reasons, I think, why she liked shopping for me more than for herself. For starters, she was overweight. Not always morbidly obese, but big enough that she usually didn't fit into the larger sizes—14, 16—offered in the regular women's sections. When I was young, there were no clothes available for her at the better department stores. She made trips to whatever special stores were necessary on her own, without me. Later, when plus sizes became readily available, she must have been embarrassed for me to know that she needed to shop in the special section. She shopped for herself the way she overate, in private.

Shopping for me, on the other hand, was like shopping for shoes. She didn't have to take her clothes off or deal with her weight, but she still had the fun of hunting and gathering, finding bargains.

We went to a set of department stores that were a twenty-minute drive away, in Garden City, Long Island. I remember the grownup-sounding click-clack of her turn signal and the patter of the radio underneath the talk about our shopping plans. There was the modern and milky white Bloomingdale's, an old fashioned Saks Fifth Avenue, and a Lord and Taylor's, where my mother liked to lunch in a restaurant on the second floor, which had a mermaid fountain stationed in the middle of the room. You had to wait to be seated. When a table became available, the hostess would hand us two oversized menus. We ordered tuna melts, sometimes cheeseburgers, with french fries when we were being bad; my mother, cottage cheese and only half a bun when she was being good.

Every couple of years, my mother returned to Weight Watcher's meetings. She baked turkey cutlets in the toaster oven and ordered steamed chicken and broccoli from Chinese restaurants with no MSG, no oil, and just soy sauce on the side. She drank Tab. She used pink-packaged saccharin in her tea. Other times she'd keep bags of pretzels and potato chips, and packages of chocolate-chip cookies and chocolate kisses and graham crackers in the kitchen pantry. After a day of teaching high school study skills and reading, she'd eat these while nodding along to Phil Donahue or Oprah, with me as often as not sitting next to her on the couch.

When we sat face to face at those Saturday department store lunches, we didn't have much to say to one another. There were the clothes, and my hair. She wanted me to comb my frizzy curls, not understanding that it was better to leave well enough alone. I'm sure she would've liked to discuss my boyfriends or love interests, but I didn't have any—none where I had a shot, anyway. We couldn't talk about my father, about what happened at home, about why she stayed. So mainly we gossiped—good-naturedly for the most part, with elongated pauses in between topics—about my friends, about my brothers and their girlfriends. Sometimes she told me about what she wore when she was my age. Penny loafers with real pennies in them, actual poodle skirts.

Sometimes her friend Dolores would come shopping with us too. Dolores was glamorous and thin, and she wore perfume and silky underwear. She would look for things for herself: fitted cream pantsuits, black cocktail dresses, tight sweaters—all in size 6 or 8. I'd sit on the sitting-room bench and watch her in wonder. Dolores didn't have a daughter.

Sometimes I was thin too. Not as thin as Dolores, but thin enough to please. Then my mother would buy me more expensive things, hoping that I'd stay that way. When I was in the eighth grade, twelve turning thirteen, I lost a lot of weight, twenty-five pounds, using the *Sweet Dreams* diet book. Around the time of my bat mitzvah, we went to Bloomingdale's, and my mother went all out and bought me a good third of the new prespring nautical resort line from Esprit. My mother had always liked me in sailor dresses. There was a navy cotton sweater with an anchor emblem patched on the chest and a canary yellow minidress with a wide cotton belt, and a red blouse with black paisley and a pair of black stirrup pants. And also a pair of brown, ankle-high, lace-up boots.

Sometimes when we came home, she'd hide the receipts from my father. Other times though, depending on how she read his mood, she'd have me give a fashion show in the family room.

By the time I was in high school, I started spending Saturdays with my friends, but still my mother continued to shop for me. She'd go to the department stores in Garden City when she had the courage to face them on her own, but more often than not she'd drive farther out to discount emporiums like Filene's Basement or Loehmann's, where shopping was more business than pleasure. She'd bring back bargains. I took these excursions of hers for granted, didn't think about what went into spending an afternoon shopping for someone else, for your daughter's body.

Back in our dining room, I'd try on skirts and tops and pants with the curtains half drawn. When something fit, my mother insisted I keep it, insisted I take one in each of two or three colors. The things were inexpensive, though occasionally she brought home an extravagant something or other. When I was a junior in high school, she purchased a couple of good wool sweaters and one that was part cashmere—with an eye, she said, for what I'd need in college.

She hit me too, but only once or twice, and not until I was a teenager. A slap on the face for being fresh; a scratch on the arm when I was disobedient. She believed in tough love, she said. She believed children had their place, that childhood was a modern-day construct, that a person of twelve should be responsible for herself.

I've always wanted a child, a girl; I've always pictured myself with a daughter. Girls, women, feel safer to me still. My daughter would never set eyes on Long Island. I'd never tell her to brush her hair or lose weight. She'd be the me I've become—nothing like my mother, nothing like the part of myself that lives there with her in the house I don't go back to anymore, not even for a tight-lipped visit, never again.

My daughter and I would go hiking, and she'd ride on my hip at Parisian flea markets and fall asleep on my lap during sitar concerts in India. She'd never be scared of her father or of me. She would know that I loved her the most, and that we'd leave the very first time.

Like my mother, I like to go clothes shopping. Something about the hunt fuels me. I don't go the big department stores; they seem old-fashioned to me now, like a general store with too many different kinds of wares.

When I want to look, I go to small shops on downtown streets, and when I want to buy, I go to high-end consignment stores, or else to the designer discount stores—the kind of places my mother used to shop for me when I was too old to want to go with her, stores with bins and color-coded discount systems I didn't have the patience for as a teenager.

My close friends who are mothers have sons, and this makes things easier between us as I long for a daughter. The one exception is my friend Paige—my friend who hates shopping, has never worn makeup or even earrings, who went searching for a wedding dress while on a solo bike trip through Vermont. (She parked her bike and tried on a dress, and that was that.) Paige likes to long-distance cross-country ski, likes to tie a canoe to the top of her station wagon and take it to the Boundary Waters. She always thought that, if she ever decided to become a parent, she'd adopt.

While living abroad in an East German university town, where her husband was a postdoc, Paige became pregnant with a daughter. I learned of the pregnancy just as Neil and I were ready to begin trying ourselves, and I was sure that I'd catch up quickly, that we'd raise our children together with Sunday brunches and summer evening bike rides. Several months later, I was pregnant too.

When the news came about my miscarriage, I didn't say anything to Paige; she was just about due and worried about giving birth in a country where she barely spoke the language. I came home from my D&C to an email about her birth story. It was long and complicated—a twenty-four-hour-plus labor and then a cesarean—not the natural birth she'd wanted. But she had her baby, a girl she named Esme.

About nine months later, we met up for a few days in Paris. While we were together, Paige wanted me to help her clothes shop. She was on a fairly strict budget while living abroad and hadn't bought anything new since the pregnancy. She wanted me to help her look like the Parisian mothers, who wore their infants like a fashion accessory. And, of course, she wanted us to shop for Esme too.

We bought Paige a black blazer and a trim pair of jeans at H&M. She spent a hundred euros, and I had to convince her to do it. But for Esme, H&M wouldn't do. We went to Le Bon Marché, the department store in the seventh arrondissement. My mouth hung open as the usually thrifty Paige considered the beautiful children's things that Esme would outgrow in months—outfits that cost as much as the wedding dress Paige had found in Vermont. She decided to splurge on a Catimini stem green dress and a pair of striped Pippi Longstocking leggings. Just what I would have chosen.

We shared a small hotel room, Paige and Esme and I. I'd picked the place—a family-run hotel in the fifth that was run down but child friendly. They had a crib to lend us, and when we came downstairs in the mornings, the owners cooed at Esme. I soon developed a strange rash on my arms and legs and belly. I thought it was a reaction to being with Esme, to witnessing mother–daughter love in the wake of my miscarriage and my subsequent trouble becoming pregnant. Lying in bed, itching in the early mornings, I'd watch Paige breastfeed. Afterward, she'd let me hold the baby. One night before dinner, Paige tied her hippie-style German *tragetuch*, or carrying towel, around me, placing Esme in the front pouch, showing me how to make the proper knots around my shoulders and hips, promising that I would need this soon, that she'd save it for me until I did.

Another nine months have gone by, and still I'm not pregnant. They can't find anything wrong with me or my husband. I've done all I can think to do on my own—acupuncture and restorative yoga and quitting drinking alcohol and caffeine for as long as I could stand it. I start treatment at the infertility clinic next month. And we are beginning to think about international adoption. In the meantime I distract myself with other kinds of love, for my husband and our dog, for my work and friends. I try to convince myself that I don't need a baby to make me happy.

But still I itch for a daughter, ache for her, dream about her. I imagine reading to her while running my short, round nails up and down her arms and along her back. I think too of the shopping excursions we'll take together. New York, Paris, Mumbai. In a land far away from Long Island, my daughter and I will make our own garden city.

Park-Bench Epiphany

**KELLY H.
JOHNSON**

"**C**hildhood is a nightmare!" declared Sheldon Kopp in his book *If You Meet the Buddha on the Road, Kill Him!* This statement is number 25 of a list of 43 items in what Kopp called an "Eschatological Laundry List" of universal truths, insights, and assorted tidbits of wisdom. I read this book for the first time when I was a sophomore in high school, and while I'm confident Mr. Kopp meant for his readers to construe the word "childhood" in a broader context, I did not. It wasn't that I didn't get the figurative meaning of the phrase. It was just that at age sixteen, "Childhood is a nightmare" struck me as a pretty accurate summation of my own experience.

I had been a skinny little girl with big eyes, bright red hair, and pale skin punctuated head to toe with freckles. Not the cute, sprinkled-over-the-nose freckles or the light smattering on forearms and shoulders, mind you, but the large, dark, crowded-in-too-small-a-space variety. Because my father was in the military, we moved around quite a bit, and with each move to a new duty station, the same sad phenomenon unfolded:

I was tormented by my peers. I was always quick to find one good friend—something that I'm certain was my saving grace—but even the most solid friendship couldn't take the sting out of being voted "most unpopular" in a fourth-grade straw poll, or protect me from the shameful chorus of children chanting "freckle face, freckle face" all the way across the playground.

When I was in fifth grade, we were stationed in northern Virginia, and there was one boy in particular—the most popular boy in school—who seemed determined to make my life miserable.

"Hey, bug-eyes. You're ugly!" he would shout in front of his friends. It was a taunt that would make them reel with laughter. And under the strain of what I now can see was intense peer pressure, even my best friend headed for higher ground, leaving me alone. At sixteen, all of this was still fresh in my mind, so when I read item number 25 in Sheldon Kopp's laundry list, I couldn't have agreed with him more.

My story has a happy ending, however. I grew up to discover that I was not a freckle-faced ugly duckling, but that I was smart and funny. I learned I was a good friend, and that my words had a way of bringing comfort to others in times of sorrow. My freckles even faded a little. These things—plus the fact that the older I got, the more distance I had between myself and my childhood—combined to strengthen my once fragile sense of self. Clichés like "What doesn't kill us makes us stronger" and "Tough times build character" became the ribbons with which I tied up my untidy childhood memories and shipped them off to long-term storage.

Life went on, and by the time I was in my early thirties, I was happily married and the mother of four sons. I assumed God must have known that a daughter would be more than I could handle. I mean, what if she looked like me? What if she had her heart broken as badly as I did? What if I had to sit by and watch her feel the pain of not being pretty enough or thin enough or *whatever* enough? No, I told myself; there was a reason I had boys.

Then I gave birth to a girl.

Looking back, I can't help wondering whether some part of my brain didn't simply shut down after she was born. It is the only explanation I can come up with for how I managed to live so blindly for the first few years of her life. I kept telling myself that I was doing great with this raising-a-girl thing, that I could handle whatever life threw at us, that I had my own girlhood memories beat. And yet I spent an inordinate amount of time that first year anxiously checking her dark hair for any hint of red. I congratulated myself with the thought that I was 100 percent over all the heartache from my childhood, ignoring the tremendous sense of relief I felt when my daughter reached her second birthday with nary a freckle. And I felt she was well on her way toward avoiding a repeat of my childhood experience when we went to the beach and she got her first tan line—something I'd never been able to achieve on my pale skin. She would be spared my fate. I was home free.

From that point forward, I was convinced that I had made it through, that the past was just that, and that the specter of my own childhood could no longer haunt me. But the fantasy came to an abrupt end on Ellery's third birthday, when her aunt casually asked her if she wanted to go to the playground.

"What's a playground?" she replied.

My heart sank. My daughter had turned three without ever having been part of a playgroup or setting foot on a playground—and that was no accident. For three years, I had kept her with me. For three years, I had come up with one reason after another to stay home: It was too hot or too cold, too crowded or too empty, too late or too early in the day. But these were merely excuses. Standing there in my kitchen with my daughter and her aunt, there was no denying that the boat with which I had so confidently sailed away from my childhood was starting to spring some pretty major leaks.

The worst part was that, while I had been perfectly content with the way things were, I knew that Ellery needed to play with other children, that she craved the company of other little girls. So two months after her third birthday, I summoned my courage and took her to the playground for the very first time.

When we arrived, she was ecstatic.

"Oh, Mama!" she gasped. "Look at all those little girls. I am going to go say hi to them, and they will like me so much!" She could hardly contain herself. I looked into her bright, expectant eyes, her little body wriggling to get out of the car seat as fast as humanly possible, and all the progress I thought I had made over the last few years vanished. A familiar anxiety began to creep over me. God give me strength, I prayed.

We walked toward the sandbox, and she immediately announced herself to the two girls playing there.

"Hi, I'm Ellery!" The girls looked up at her and then resumed their playing. "Hi, I'm Ellery!" she said again, taking a few steps onto the sand. Still nothing. I could feel a knot beginning to form in my stomach. She bent down next to one of the girls. "What's your name?" she asked.

"Brianna," the girl answered.

Okay, I thought. Maybe this will be alright.

"I'm Ellery," she repeated for a third time. "Do you want to play with me?"

My blood pressure skyrocketed. *Please say yes, please say yes!*

"No," Brianna answered and got up and walked to the other side of the sandbox.

Ellery knelt down beside the second girl. "What's your name?" she asked. The little girl just looked at her. Ellery tried one last time. Still, silence. Meanwhile, I was fighting my impulse to rescue her, trying instead to wait this out, to see if she needed me. Ellery seemed more confused by what was happening than anything else. But I was already projecting ten years into the future, imagining her having to work out self-esteem issues that surely could be traced back to this interaction in the sandbox.

"Mama, she's not talking," she said to me.

"Maybe she's shy, honey," I offered. "Why don't you play by yourself for a minute." She looked entirely unsatisfied with this, but she gave it a try. I, on the other hand, was unraveling. I felt weak and uneasy and desperate to leave.

It wasn't long before she tired of her solitary play and headed to the slide, where a group of girls her age had gathered, waiting for their turns. I walked to the closest bench and sat down. I looked at Ellery, all smiles and happy expectation, and I was painfully aware that by contrast, I was virtually cowering in a corner. *What am I so afraid of?* I asked myself. *Look at her! She is joyous, sparkling, thrilled to be here.* I tried to focus on the joy that was so apparent on her face, on her exuberant glances in my direction as she inched her way to the front of the line. But nothing could stop the familiar reel of "what ifs" that had started playing in my head: *What if she gets her feelings hurt for real next time? What if, next time, there is still no one who wants to play?* My head began to hurt, my throat felt tight, and suddenly I was eight years old, back on the school playground. *You cannot do this to her,* I admonished myself. *You cannot bring her into this web of insecurity and fear.* I had reached a crossroads and I knew it.

It is so hard not to superimpose my own childhood struggles onto my daughter. Even when I try my hardest, it is just so easy to go astray. There is no question that I worried a great deal about my boys when they were Ellery's age, but nothing like this. While we didn't exactly blaze new trails in toddler socialization, we got out far more often than Ellery and I ever did—not that it mattered to them. My boys couldn't have cared less about meeting other children; for them, playtime was always about trucks and trains and dirt and more dirt. Looking back, I am convinced that it was their indifference to playmates that kept my childhood demons at bay.

My daughter was another story, however. From the moment she could put two syllables together, Ellery excelled at the art of conversation. She babbled incessantly and in dramatic fashion to us, to the faces on the TV, and to countless other folks, real and imagined. She greeted everyone who caught her eye—grandmothers, teenagers, babies, and the occasional dog—with the same brimming enthusiasm. And when they smiled back at her, as they almost always did, it seemed to confirm to her that this was indeed a world of great kindness and all she had to do was to wait for the magic to unfold. I loved this about her. I admired it, really. But I knew the world could be terribly unkind, and I was terrified that her fall would be precipitous. *Just a little longer,* I kept telling myself. *Shield her just a little longer.* And before I knew it, she was three.

The irony is that even before she was born, I was aware of the mothers at my sons' elementary school, who, on the surface at least, seemed to be trying to live their unrealized dreams through their daughters. I took great pains to not make *that* mistake. But it has proven impossible to resist the sway of gender, its siren song that calls to mind my own experience as my daughter makes her way on the path to womanhood. As it turns out, my problem doesn't seem to be in my trying to live through her. It's in my trying to allow her to live.

As I sat there on that bench watching my daughter, I could no longer ignore what was becoming so obvious: My efforts to save Ellery from experiencing the kind of pain I had endured were inexorably linked with a frantic desire to save the little girl within me as well. I had known all the right things to say to comfort that little girl; I had told myself a thousand times that hard times build character and that my pain had made me who I was. But I hadn't really believed it. In a moment, I finally understood. To fully accept my past, I had to confront the silent wish that I carried around for almost my entire life: I wanted a different childhood.

Slowly, tenderly, I allowed myself to acknowledge this wish and to admit, finally, that it was still there, aching to be fulfilled. Then I waited. Far from feeling any relief, I felt embarrassed that my hurt and shame was still so raw, that such a yearning would persist so strongly within me after all these years. But sitting there on that park bench in a state of utter vulnerability, I experienced a moment of profound grace.

I saw that buried within my desire for a less painful past was the presumption that I would remain exactly the person I am in the present. And in that grace-filled moment I realized the futility of that desire. My childhood was the way to the here and now, to who I am today. My childhood—not another. All this time, I had been asking to be a tulip that grew from a daisy seed or a diamond that wasn't once a lump of coal. All this time, I had wanted to be me—without having actually been me.

And so I made a vow. I would force myself to keep bringing Ellery to playgrounds and play dates. I would enjoy the good days and tough it out with her on the bad days. I would do this, despite the ulcers it might cause me, because I know that Ellery's experience—her suffering, her joy, her heartache, her laughter, whatever befalls her—will be the dirt and the sun, the air and the water that nourishes the seed of her soul. I know she must be allowed the chance to harvest her life's wisdom for herself.

As I gathered my things to leave the park bench, I took a long look at Ellery running merrily around the playground, and I saw that she was no longer playing alone. A petite girl with long blonde hair was racing along beside her, squealing with delight. I put my things down and sat on the bench. With a full heart I watched them run, hand in hand, their laughter carried on the wind like prayers offered up to heaven.

A Strong Baby Girl

EMILY ALEXANDER STRONG

We wanted to conceive.

The trip was a sweaty, dirty, exhausting, exhilarating ride down the coast of the south island of New Zealand to Queenstown, then back up the opposite coast to Blenheim, our home base. It was February, the Southern Hemisphere's summer, so my husband and I spent most nights in the one-person tent we shared. Each morning we put on the same clothes from the day before: ripe-smelling jerseys, bike shorts, and socks crusty with yesterday's sweat. We pulled our belongings in trailers behind our touring bikes.

Imagining the babies we'd create was my favorite pastime as I pedaled, well behind Eric, up the toughest hills. My psyche produced vague offspring, but I knew any child of mine would be strong and athletic, would roughhouse with their dad, and would sport at least one Band-Aid on a skinned knee all summer long. For girls, the names were androgynous. Harper, Piper, Ryann, Carter. Lorin, my great-grandfather's name. Looking back on it, I was naming a tomboy; I just didn't realize it.

With each rotation of the pedals, my quads hardened, my tan darkened, and my confidence, like the mercury in the thermometers displayed at some Kiwi petrol stations, climbed upward. I felt invincible, sporty, sexy—my favorite self.

I was pregnant before we got home.

On December 30, 2000, we welcomed a little girl into the world. Her birth announcement, a play on our last name, read "A Strong Baby Girl Is Born." We decorated her nursery in yellow and green with a farm-animal motif. Eric and I would not impose froufrou, girly stuff on her. After all, we had both grown up listening to *Free to Be You and Me*.

For a good two-and-a-half years, Eliza—named after a favorite cousin rather than one of the gender-neutral picks I envisioned on our trip—was the kind of girl I wanted her to be. I dressed her in hand-me-down overalls and let her natural curls tangle. When my sister Margaret, a mother of two boys, bought Eliza the pinkest, girliest frock she could find for Christmas, I thanked her but was careful not to wrinkle the tissue paper so I could regift it to one of my more estrogen-happy friends. We had no time for dresses and tea parties. In our coastal town of Mendocino, California, we spent hours on the rugged beaches dragging seaweed, drawing in the sand, and jumping off rocks.

One day, out on the rocky beach, Eliza lost her balance and landed awkwardly on her wrist. We rode, without a tear, to the emergency room, where we discovered her radius and ulna were broken. For the next six weeks, she hauled her casted arm up and over those same rocks. When the doctor cut the cast off, sand, twigs, and leaves fell out. "A real nature baby, eh?" the doctor remarked.

"Yeah," I beamed.

It turned out those first years were the easy ones, with her as the roughhousing tomboy I'd envisioned. But as Eliza got older, it became obvious that she was small for her age. This shouldn't have meant anything to me, but it did: She was dainty. Petite. Her peers towered over her. When we went to the pediatrician's office for her four-year well check, her stature was confirmed with a mark on a growth chart. Trying not to hover, I winced as a nurse, her fingernails red with white flowers, guided her pen from dot to dot. Eliza's growth curve, once overlapping the dark red "average" line, had lost stream, falling progressively farther and farther away from a number I inexplicably wanted for her. Even after the doctor told me that there was no need to worry, that she was just taking her time growing, I felt a pull in my stomach, like a tugged-on thread that bunches the hem of a skirt. "Small but mighty!" I said to the doctor with a stiff smile, then laughed a little too loudly.

That day, I rode to the park with Eliza. Strapping her in the five-point harness, it struck me that she, at twenty-nine pounds, weighed less than the gear I'd hauled through New Zealand. I ruminated as I rode, just as I had on our trip, though this time, the setting was our new home, the storybook town of Ashland, Oregon. I tried to brush off the discomfort I'd felt at the doctor's office. "Hell," I said out loud to myself, "those dumb charts are derived from kids whose parents feed them McDonald's for breakfast, lunch, and dinner." I felt smug at my defiance of mainstream America as Eliza and I rolled into Lithia Park, a lovely playground bordered by a creek fresh and full from the spring runoff.

I unclipped Eliza's harness and helmet as she wiggled impatiently. She ran to see Uma, a girl just one month older than herself but a head taller. As Uma's hug lifted Eliza's feet off the ground, Eliza wrapped her legs around Uma's hips. Uma's baby sitter, whom we had not met before, commented.

"Eliza is sooo cute! Is she Brian's age?" Brian—Uma's two-year-old brother.

"No," I corrected her, "Eliza is Uma's age. She's four." I was tempted to point out that Eliza no longer had the proportions of a toddler, that she did not have a bulky diaper bottom, and that her fluid movements were of a coordinated little girl, but I bit my tongue.

Holding hands, Uma and Eliza ran over to the swings. With the chain of the swing in each hand, Uma pulled herself up and popped her bottom onto the swing. Eliza attempted the same, her hands reaching the chain only slightly above the seat. She bent her arms, suspending her body, but the seat hit the middle of her back.

"Mom, I can't—get—up here!" she said between grunts.

I gave Eliza a little lift. She looked crestfallen. "It's not fair, Mom. Uma can do so much stuff that I can't."

And the tug in my stomach returned.

Still, her size didn't seem to slow her down; if anything, it was more of an issue for me than it was for her. But when she started preschool, the experience was hard on us both. At the beginning of the school year, I was comforted that my child was not the only one having trouble saying goodbye to Mom. But as the school's bulletin-board displays changed with the seasons, I watched other kids—even those who at first wept at dropoff—wrangle out of their mother's grip to join friends without even a "See ya, Mom!" over their shoulders. With Eliza, every goodbye until winter vacation was a scene of tears and pleading.

"But Mom, I just like being with you!" she'd wail as I'd pry her clenched fingers from my wrist. Then I'd get in my station wagon, start the engine, and cry myself. I had seen the looks from some of the more mature girls who sat at the coloring table. Looks that said, "Eliza is such a cry baby!" Once I actually heard a girl (who happened to be wearing a dress-up tiara) say "Not Eliza again" as my daughter went into her daily hysterics. Did girls really snub each other as early as preschool? When I told my sister about the comment, she jokingly offered to come over and "kick some preschool butt."

We laughed, but I was concerned that Eliza was considered the baby of the class because of her size and behavior. Finally, in January, when the crying stopped, the teachers began to comment, "She is so articulate! So verbal!" I thanked them but wanted to hiss, "You're only finding this out now?"

Even at home, there were times when Eliza's sensitivity shocked me. One afternoon, desperate to talk on the phone with my newly-in-love best friend in London, I put on a video to entertain Eliza. I picked *Maisy,* about an innocuous cartoon mouse who has adventures with a squirrel, an elephant, an alligator, and a chicken named Tallulah. Two minutes into hearing about the love of my friend's life—"He is it, Ems," Lisa told me breathlessly—I heard a panicked scream: "Mom, I don't like this part! Go past it!"

Could the video have turned off, switched over to TV; could she be suddenly witnessing a murder? The urgency in her voice suggested it, but I knew my daughter too well. I asked Lisa to hold on, frustrated that costly time was ticking.

"I don't like when they go through the dark tunnel. Sit with me!"

"I can't honey. I'm talking to Lisa, my friend who lives across the ocean? It's really important."

"But I need you mom! Sit with me!"

I tried to appease Eliza, but it wasn't working. She was getting more hysterical by the minute.

"Lisa, this isn't going to work. I'm so sorry. Maybe I can call tomorrow?"

"MOM!"

I hung up, livid. I wanted to scream that this video was intended for two-year-olds and that she was four, that she was watching a happy little train full of animated creatures, not something frightening. I wanted to tell her she was being a wimp, a scaredy-cat.

But I didn't. Instead I let her cuddle up to me as she rhythmically sucked her thumb and fingered a blankie that was a shadow of its former self due to her habit of pulling out the strings. She was truly scared.

I said, "I'll watch this part with you, honey. I know the dark can be scary."

My nose tingled, a warning that tears were threatening. Why was it so hard for me to accept that my little girl was a little girl both physically and emotionally? I knew for sure that I was not an ice queen.

And that's when it all started to make sense.

What disappoints me is not that Eliza has fears and sensitivities. Her fragility scares me because I know it all too well.

As a child I was extremely sensitive. When I was eleven years old, just before my parents told us—their three children—that they would be getting a divorce, I was wound so tight that a snap from my brother's cap gun startled me out of my skin and sent me into loud, uncontrolled tears. I remember the fear in my mother's eyes as she looked at me and rocked me like a baby in her too-thin arms. Over the years, I learned to hide my sensitivity because it made others as uncomfortable as it had made my mother. Like the layer upon layer of finish that my woodworker husband applies to his furniture, I gradually hardened my exterior.

While playing high school and college soccer, I was a fierce competitor on the outside, yet more than once, I fought back tears after an opponent's goal. I'd return to the center line, wiping away the salt of tears and sweat with the crook of my elbow, and vow not to let the other team score again. During those same years, I studied biology. Later, when I taught the subject to middle-schoolers, I felt part of my job was to be a role model for young women. Even though most of my female students would squeal as I demonstrated the dissection of a sheep eye (the boys wanted to squeal, but didn't), I knew it was important for them to see a woman in a lab coat, using a scalpel skillfully to reveal the cornea, lens, and optic nerve. They did not need to know that I have squeamish moments myself, or that I refuse to eat lamb because I hate that it is killed so young.

Until Eliza was born, I had successfully masked my inner wimp with a facade of strength and confidence. But now I have a daughter who seems to insist on wearing my heart on her sleeve.

I know for certain I can't change Eliza's sensitive nature. I know it only feels worse when somebody tries to. I know it feels especially bad when that somebody is your mother. I never want Eliza to feel there is something wrong with her beautiful little self. Because, of course, there isn't.

Now when Eliza's alert antennae tell her something doesn't feel right, I try to ignore the tug in my stomach and listen to her instead. Last week we were behind stage at a children's festival, waiting for her dance class to perform. Her teacher Gene, stressed and frazzled, was shouting directions to the mass of tutus and ponytails crowded in the wings. "I need my choo-choo train kids over here! You're on next! Parents, please stop talking!" Behind us, a stage mom mouthed the words and did the hand gestures for the "Wind the Bobbin" song in a desperate attempt to prep her three-year-old. As she stuck out her elbows to wind a giant invisible bobbin, she struck Eliza in the temple. Eliza had already been on edge about performing; this decided it.

"I don't want to do it!" she said.

"I don't blame you," I said as I swept her onto my hip and out the back door. We walked around to the front of the outdoor stage and sat on a knoll to view the performance. As the dancers entered and parents set their video cameras on record, I pulled Eliza onto my lap and squeezed her tightly. I then told her what I knew to be true: that by listening to her own voice, she was the bravest of them all.

My strong baby girl.

Links

JENNIFER
LAUCK

Three AM shadows come through the slats of the window blind. Out the window, streetlights shine amber circles on the wet and empty street. A row of maples are bare of leaves, and their branches reach high like old women's skinny arms with so many questions.

I hold Josephine, and her baby weight molds into the deflated soft of my stomach.

In our room, there is a narrow bed with metal railings to keep us from falling, a side table on wheels that holds a box of tissues, and a water bottle that has the words "Providence Hospital" printed on clear plastic. Across the room, there is the shape of the television suspended from the ceiling and, against the wall, more shapes of the sofa, a chair, a round table, and two more chairs. Other than Josephine, me, and the teddy bear that my son Spencer sent to get us safely through our first night, we are alone with the furniture and the shadows.

An hour ago, we weren't alone. An hour ago, this room was full of people and light.

An hour ago, Josephine was being born, more and more of her emerging each time I grabbed my breath and pushed. Steve lifted my leg, his way of helping. He said he couldn't believe I was so strong.

Our strength is also our weakness.

The big muscles of my legs were powerful, but the subtle ones, the ones the Indians call the *bandhas*, were small and weak. In bringing my baby through my body, I had to learn to channel power from my legs to those other places, and each time I got it wrong, Josephine retreated, and I had to try again. It took a long time.

A nurse named Jill stood nearby, giving instructions on how to hold my breath and count inside my head. The doctor named Alice sat in an easy chair with her legs crossed, so casual, so relaxed.

"You're doing great," Alice said. "Don't rush, take your time."

When I got it all right, the breathing, the pushing, the shifting of power within, Josephine finally emerged through the ring of fire, a soft, sticky, white baby.

Jill and Alice and Steve and I cried and laughed and looked at one another.

"Oh my god, it's amazing, isn't it?"

Real miracles have a way of stealing verbal eloquence.

In that speechless space, Josephine was given over to me and laid on top of my chest. She was so sturdy and strong, and I folded her into myself, as perfect a fit on the outside as she had been on the inside.

For a while, there was the fussing around that goes with a new baby, the weighing and the measuring and the testing for reflexes. When Josephine wasn't with me, she cried, and as soon as she was back in the solid fit of my arms, she stopped.

Then Alice left to deliver twins.

Jill said goodbye, too. It was the end of her shift.

Steve went home to get some sleep.

The room cleared of people and sound, the light was turned off, and the door swung to a close.

I could have gone to sleep; my body certainly needed the rest. Josephine had already gone to a place that only babies seem to go, two fingers in her mouth as she nodded her chin against her chest.

I couldn't sleep, though; I had this feeling there was a visitor in the shadows. It was this woman who came to call on me, this woman who needed to talk. She said now that Josephine was here and sleeping against my heart, it was time to take a trip with her to the other side.

I once had a friend named Patty. She was small, with a wide smile on a moon-round face. Her last name should have been Pie; she was that cute. We lived across the hall from each other, twenty-year-old girls in their first apartments. There was a familiar quality to Patty. It was there in the lost look of her round, soft eyes, and after we talked for a while, I found out what the familiar thing was. She had been adopted when she was born, just like me.

We were sitting on the stoop of our apartments, drinking longneck beers without anywhere to go. Once the "adopted" thing was out there, we were like best friends.

"Did your real mother get to hold you?" Patty said.

I took a swig of my beer and shook my head.

"I don't think so," I said.

"How do you know?" she said.

"Someone told me I got taken to the nursery right away. Then my parents, Bud and Janet, got me three days later," I said. "How about you?"

Patty leaned with her elbows on her knees and she held her beer by the neck, letting it swing back and forth. She had a far-off look in her eyes.

"I think she held me," Patty said.

I looked in the direction Patty looked, but over there, it was just more apartments like ours, a street, and a few trees.

"How do you know?" I said.

Patty turned to me and smiled this secret smile.

"I just know," she said. "I can feel it in my body."

I watched her for such a long time. I had no idea what she meant by that, and I tried to feel into my own body for that kind of thing. In me was a kind of emptiness that, if you looked at it long enough, would turn into tears. I drank down the rest of my beer.

Patty wasn't on her own and living across the hall from me for very long before she told me that she had to find her first mother. Her second mother was a good woman—Patty loved her with almost all of her heart—but something was missing.

Patty's talk of her first mother couldn't make its way past my ears and into my heart. I couldn't understand it. I couldn't feel it. Thinking about it just made me mad. Adoption was the ultimate rejection. My first mother didn't want me, and to make that okay, I wouldn't let myself want to know anything about her.

Patty made calls and was told to write a letter. There was a file in a drawer at the agency, and in that file, another letter was waiting. The letters fit together to make a whole, and just like that, Patty found her real mother. Right away, they were reunited, a family of Patty Pies, small people with wide smiles on moon-round faces. They were cute and happy and their story went like this:

Patty's mother was a teenager, and her parents sent her to a place where girls give up their babies. It was a Catholic girls' school in Spokane. Patty's mother had Patty, and the nuns let her hold her baby for a whole night. Patty's mom loved her too much to give her up, but she had no money and nowhere to go. In the morning, a nun took Patty away, and Patty's mom went back to her life as a daughter living on a farm. Two years later, Patty's mom married Patty's dad and made a family beyond Patty, always longing for her though, always wanting her back.

Way back when I was about eleven years old, I was sent to live with my aunt after Janet, and then Bud, died. There were a bunch of legal papers that came with me, stuff about my Social Security benefits and life insurance and other things my aunt didn't let me see. She did give me a small rectangle of paper though. It wasn't a whole sheet; it was just half a page, and it had a raised seal that read "The State of Nevada." In the lines under the seal, there were typewriter words that put together the details of my first mother and my first father.

I took that page and folded it in half, then in half again, and then in half one more time and slid it between the pages of an encyclopedia that I kept on my desk. I'd unfold that paper and memorize the lines of how my first mother was small-boned and French, and how my first father had dark eyes and dark skin. The lines on that piece of paper held the promise of something familiar, if only in features, and they gave tastes of comfort that come from the idea of family. I liked to close my eyes and imagine people out there who looked like me, who were maybe looking for me too.

After I grew up and moved out of my aunt and uncle's house, I stopped looking at that piece of paper. I kept it stored in the encyclopedia and kept the encyclopedia locked in my trunk. But Patty's reunion with her mother teased me to dig it out and make a telephone call.

A nice woman in Nevada explained the procedure. I write a letter, they open a file, and if my first mother or my first father wrote a letter too, our letters would make a match.

"Then we'll call you and make arrangements," she said, very professional, very polite.

I thought about it for such a long time, my heart like a small child begging candy from a grownup. Just write, what can it hurt to write? Of course my mother is waiting for me. Who knows how many years her letter has been waiting in a dusty file. Just write. Just write.

I wrote the letter and I waited. I waited and I waited. While I waited, I checked the telephone for a dial tone. I looked at it whenever I walked by, and when I couldn't wait another day, I called.

"Yes," the woman said, very professional, very polite. "We received your letter, but no, there are no other letters here yet. We'll call you."

I don't keep in touch with Patty anymore. She has her family now.

I don't have that half-sheet of paper, either; it got lost in all the times I've moved.

I have called the State of Nevada three times to tell them I've changed my address. I made those calls from Montana, then Washington, and finally Oregon, and they were like whispers of hope crossing state lines from where I was to where my first mother might be waiting. But she never was.

Perhaps she is dead.

Perhaps she forgot.

Perhaps she never wants to remember.

I gave up thinking about her at all. You can't live your life staring at the telephone.

But with Josephine in my arms, her strong, new heartbeat against my own (not so strong and not so new anymore), the whispers in the shadows prove that sometimes you think you've given up but you haven't, not really. How could I forget the woman who brought me into the world? How could I not think about her on days like my birthday or on a day like this, when I hold my brand new daughter in my arms?

In the way that you can only imagine at 3:00 AM, I let myself fall into the possibility of my first mother. Our story went like this: My birth had been complicated. Forceps pulled me from her, and when it was over, I was wrapped up and taken away. Patty's mom held her all night long, but my mother didn't get her baby. That's the way it was done in Nevada.

When Spencer was born premature, he was taken away from me so the doctors could perform a bunch of tests in a room I couldn't get to for a few hours. Not being able to have him in my arms shredded my heart down to its core.

I could feel the emptiness of my own mother's arms on the night I was born, and if I could feel all that and see to the past, could I go one more step? Could I send a message over the waves of time between now and then; could I say, "I have a daughter now. She's here and she's beautiful, and in holding her I am healing all of us, at least a little bit"?

Dawn dissolves the dark, and the clock rounds past five, but I am still between now and then, and my message flows out to my real mother, wherever she was. Perhaps she would get it in a dream and wake up to the memory of me, that daughter she never held but never forgot, or that daughter she did forget until the dream woke her up. Perhaps she was dead but her soul wandered days and nights, in search of answers that only time could give, until finally she got one more that she could add to her collection before traveling on to other spirit places.

By six, the dark is gone and it's raining. The silence on the empty street has been sliced away by the spray of tires, cars full of people going to work and school and wherever else they need to go. One woman walks under the bare maple trees, her head hidden under the curve of her wide black umbrella.

Josephine stirs against me and takes a deep breath into her nose. She opens her eyes long enough to see me still awake, still watching her, and nods as if to say, "Yes, you're still here." She closes her eyes again, going back to rest and recover and rebuild after her long journey.

The shadows are gone. It is a new day. I close my eyes, and sleep moves over me right away. I didn't realize I was so tired.

On Wanting a Girl

**SHARI MACDONALD
STRONG**

During the first half of our pregnancy, when interested parties ask what my husband and I hope we are having—boy or girl—I laugh with the confidence of a woman who has worked too long and too hard not to have things turn out her way now.

"The politically correct thing is to say, 'As long as the baby's healthy . . .'" I admit. "And it's true. But—" I lean in, as if I am about to reveal an honest-to-goodness secret, "I'm also hoping for a girl. And Craig wants a boy. He's the last male in his family, you know. It's up to him to carry on the name." I add this last bit to be charitable, as if my spouse's desire for a same-sex child needs some defense. My own preference— born, it seems, of my experience as a woman and feminist—presumably needs no justification.

When we announce that we have more than one child on the way, friends suggest, "Maybe you'll get both!"

"Maybe," I say, uncharacteristically coy. I already envision a nursery full of girls with dark curls, candy pink dresses, and chubby fingers like sausages just right for nibbling; small beauties who will grow into impossible teenage girls, known in the neighborhood for their overflowing bookshelves, brilliant minds, emerging activist sensibility, and damn good hair.

From the moment we learn that the in vitro attempt has been a spectacular success (out of four embryos—three healthy and one slow developer—75 percent of our test-tube offspring have "taken" in our friend's supremely hospitable womb), I know that my long-dreamt-of daughter is on her way to me. I feel certain of it the day our reproductive endocrinologist confirms the pregnancy; our surrogate, my husband, and I stare in silence at grainy, black-and-white images on a monitor mounted above the hospital bed as the doctor points out three separate heartbeats: rapid and delicate, the flutter of moths' wings, our first real evidence of life.

A spiritually intuitive friend tells me that among the babies, we have at least one child of each gender. I suspect, or perhaps merely wish for, two girls and a boy. Yes, one boy would be fine, just fine. I can afford to be magnanimous concerning my husband's dream as I do not doubt that my own will come true.

At our ten-week appointment, the doctor can no longer find Baby A's heartbeat.

As my friend's womb reabsorbs my baby's body, I dance with my loss—one moment, wailing like the wounded animal I am; the next, denying that I'm allowed to feel bad for more than a week or, at most, two. I am profoundly saddened though, and terribly shaken—even though we still have two babies on the way, even though a risky triplet pregnancy is more than our surrogate bargained for, even though we are just ten weeks into this long-awaited pregnancy by proxy. I fear for Craig too; I worry that the boy he wants is gone. It occurs to me that Baby A may have been a daughter, but I cannot face this possibility and dismiss it as too unlikely to seriously consider.

In June, six days before my thirty-fifth birthday, a technician slathers our surrogate's bulky, baby-full belly with gel, prods her overstretched skin with an ultrasound wand, and announces that Baby B is, without a doubt, a member of the testosterone club.

I could not be more shocked. "Honey!" I cry to my husband, who is sitting with me at the surrogate's side. "You got your boy!" For a moment, I am thrilled for the man I love. Then, for the first time, I feel nervous.

"And," says the technician many long, agonizing minutes later, "you have . . . another boy!"

"What?" I say. Then again. *What?*

I do my best to act excited in front of our surrogate, who I cannot bear to have see me as ungrateful. Then, fooling no one, I excuse myself to the restroom where I drop to the linoleum and sob for several minutes before returning to husband, friend, and technician—none of whom I can bear to look in the eye, but who I sense are all throwing pitying glances my way. When our little group finally leaves the ultrasound room, the technician gives me several printouts of the evidence. At home, I deposit the blurry black-and-white images on top of the stereo with exaggerated carelessness, then barely glance at them again for more than a week. Every time I walk past, I imagine the two little penises waving at me like smug little flags: profoundly startling, entirely other, mocking me with their very existence.

My therapist suggests that I want to mother a daughter because I long to go back in time to reparent the wounded young girl that was me.

I think, *What does he know about it? He has a penis too.*

In the months that follow, I come to uneasy terms with the gender of my soon-to-arrive children. I pack up countless piles of tiny, girly dresses that I can't bear to sell or give away and begin the process of replacing them with blue, white, and yellow onesies.

Fall arrives, and shortly thereafter, so do my sons. The instant they make their entrance, I fall in love. By the time I find a moment to stop and think about it (for the first few weeks, I barely can take time to pee), I can no longer remember what it felt like to wish they were anything other than exactly what they are.

The emotion I feel for my boys makes the most generous love I had envisioned seem pale and worthless. But even as my maternal affection swells, so does my stubborn desire for a daughter. There is no part of me that wants a girl *instead of* the boys; suddenly this is about *in addition to*.

I return to the adoption photo listings on the Internet, which I pored over even as we were pursuing surrogacy. My husband and I had agreed that our next child would be a daughter we adopt from overseas, something we planned to do perhaps next year.

It is the tendency of both our babies to sleep half the day away; the trick is getting them to sleep at the same time. Their leisure time is spent listening to my husband or me read excerpts from Harold Bloom's *Stories and Poems for Extremely Intelligent Children of All Ages,* swatting at primary-color toys hanging from the zebra-striped bar of their baby gym, and watching our shepherd mix circle them with a look of "Dear God, what are those things?" on her doggy face. The babies do not appear bored. I definitely am not. But I am already consumed with the existence of our boys' sister and am plotting how we will find her and bring her home.

I identify her by photograph almost instantly: with her wide brown eyes, apple-shaped face, and chestnut hair, she is the very image of me at age one. She is exactly as I imagined her. Moved by his love for me and by my sense of urgency, my startled husband agrees to travel with me to Russia to meet Ksenia. We call the agency and commit to her. Between diaper changes, formula feedings, and laundry, I complete massive volumes of paperwork. I feel myself attaching to Ksenia at a base, core maternal level, just as I have done with the boys. I get our home study started and arrange for friends and family to cover a full week of infant childcare. I retrieve colorful 18m-size sleepers and dresses from the basement, where they have been banished along with the girls' 6Ms, 12Ms, 2Ts, 3Ts, and 4Ts accumulated early in the pregnancy. I engage in a heated internal debate about whether we should keep Ksenia's given name or change it to Daisy, our top choice when the boys were still in utero. I buy a doll for Ksenia; bath salts and wristwatches for the orphanage caretakers. I imagine our new little family together constantly.

Three days before we are to get on the plane to go meet our new daughter, I have our airline tickets, visas, and passports in hand. The adoption agency calls, but it is not to confirm travel plans, as I expect. I am told that Ksenia's birth mother has contacted the Russian orphanage to say that she is coming back to take Ksenia home.

I try to imagine what I can do. I am desperate. *There must be some way to stop this*, I think. But how can I want any other outcome for this girl if I genuinely care about her? I try to tell myself that, at least to me, she will always be my daughter. But I know this isn't true; she already has a mother, and it isn't me.

And anyway, the adoption agency tells me a week later, she is already gone.

"How do you feel?" my therapist would say if I had the time or the financial resources to consult him now.

I feel like I haven't just lost my daughter, I have lost a piece of myself. I feel like I may be losing my mind.

Now in possession of our nonrefundable deposit, the adoption agency sends us a photograph of a girl who appears to be a young two but is in fact almost three. She has sandy hair, hazel eyes, and wears an expression I gauge to be something between suspicion and innocence. She is wearing a rose-colored dress over bare, mildly bowed legs and clutches a Hello Kitty doll still trapped in its packaging, hers to hold on this occasion alone. It is a donation to the orphanage—never played with, the special toy of no child. I want to get excited about this girl, but I am physically and emotionally drained.

Though she is enough like me physically that we could be related by blood, she does not look like Ksenia. Nor does she so closely resemble the child I was a long time ago. I put off watching the referral video from the orphanage, but when I finally do, her funny little personality charms me.

"Oooh, she's a little *cheese*burger," says my spiritually intuitive friend, watching the videotape with me.

On the video, the girl enters the playroom and sits at a child-size table, where her Russian caregivers have placed several puzzles so that she may prove to the family represented by the camera just how fine a catch she is. She eyes the videographer warily, flashing a look that clearly says, *I certainly hope you don't think I'm doing all this for you.*

She does not cling to the adults or beg for attention, nor does she shuffle off unsociably. She seems remarkably intact despite all she's gone through—it is doubtful that I will ever find out what all that entails. Her roguish half-smirk is surprisingly endearing. She strikes me as a bit of a smartass. I like that in a girl.

I tell my husband we should go get her. He thinks I am crazy. He is not the only one.

Taking our cue from Quaker friends, my husband and I call for a Meeting for Clearness: a group practice designed to help in the discernment of God's will. Though we are not Quakers ourselves and hardly know how to lead such a gathering, we are hungry for any bit of wisdom we can appropriate. The idea of sitting in silence with those we love suits us, and we find solace in the perceived safety of making our decision within the bosom of community.

My husband says that I would make a good Quaker, if it weren't for what he calls "the silence thing." He is referring to the value given to silence in Quaker worship; but as a recovering religious conservative who was for years expected to keep dissenting opinions to herself, I take this observation as a fabulous compliment and repeat it often to anyone I wish to impress or, in the case of particularly conservative friends, shock and horrify.

Craig and I briefly present our dilemma to our small gathering of loved ones—should we adopt this little girl? Then we all sit together quietly, listening, waiting for God to speak to our hearts.

Sitting cross-legged on our friends' living room floor, I strain against the silence, trying to make out God's voice. Is Eugenia meant to be ours?

Long minutes pass, but no answers come to me in the quiet stillness; only another question: *Can you let her be who she is?* I am disappointed, thinking that we have come up empty. No one in the room feels strongly led in one way or the other. The decision is up to my husband and me.

We leap.

Eight months and two trips to Russia later, we are the parents of two baby boys and a preschool-age daughter. My husband and I have gone from having no children to having three under the age of four, in just under a year.

"Wow, you guys sure have your hands full!" people say with a laugh when they meet us. Our family possesses the power to turn every man and woman into a master of understatement.

It turns out that Eugenia is nothing like the carbon copy of me I was shooting for. As a child, I treated books like sacred artifacts; she views every one as her own personal coloring book, an approach that has left the personal library I have been building for thirty-seven years profoundly worse for the wear. In my youth, I was nervous and dreamy; Eugenia is a magnificent specimen of volume, intensity, and hardheadedness. Where as I was an incurable people-pleaser, she is stubborn and profoundly independent. "How can I deal with her misbehavior if she doesn't respond to guilt?" I grumped at my husband one day. "It's the only discipline skill I inherited from my parents."

I remember the melancholy I felt when I learned we were having sons. *Boys? What does a person do with boys, anyway?* Back then, I felt confident about having girls; I had experience in this area, or so I thought. It turns out that the only thing I really had experience with, though, was me. And Eugenia isn't anymore *me* than the boys are—or, for that matter, than is anyone else.

Back in my therapist's office (finances no longer my most pressing concern), I agonize over Eugenia's sheer strength of will. I tell him it wasn't what I had in mind.

"You've always wanted a chance to raise a strong daughter," he observes. "You just hoped that she would be dysfunctional and weak first, so you could fix her."

One afternoon, my daughter, now five years old, finds me sitting on the couch, leafing through Hillary Clinton's memoir.

"What's that, Mama?" she asks, climbing on top of me in the general area of my full bladder.

"It is the story of a strong woman," I say, scooting her forty-some-odd pounds farther back in my lap, onto my legs. "A woman who a lot of people don't like."

"Why?" This is my daughter's favorite word, and she believes in using it indiscriminately and often.

"Because she doesn't act how other people tell her a woman should act." I am gratified to have this opportunity to raise up for her an example of women's power. "She doesn't care what other people think. She does whatever she believes is right and best."

"I don't care what other people think," she informs me. "I do what I want to do." She says this as if the fact might actually come as a surprise to me.

"Yes, I know, sweetie." I roll my eyes. "Caving in to other people will never be your problem." The way I say it leaves unspoken words hanging in the air: *You will have other problems, because you are strong-willed, and you do not listen.* Not noticing, she laughs and clamors across my lap. In an instant I realize that I am holding something truly sacred: a brilliant, budding, woman-in-the-making, my daughter. And I am glad that this time, I chose silence.

My friend who does metaphysical readings tells me that before children's souls enter this world, the children choose their future parents. They do this knowing what hardships and struggles they will face in their family of origin—and thus knowing what lessons they must learn again and again, throughout their lives. She says that Eugenia knew she would be adopted, and that she also chose me for her mother—just as, almost two years ago, I chose her.

"You have a lot of love to give," my friend tells me, "but you have always struggled with your power. You are going to teach Eugenia about unconditional love. And she is going to teach you about being a woman of power.

"It is why you are together. This is your gift."

It is an hour past bedtime, and I am singing lullabies to my children—or trying to. My daughter interrupts repeatedly with details about her day at her Montessori preschool, until I finally give up and quit the song I am singing.

"Okay, tell me what you want to tell me," I say to her from my rocking chair, "but I'm done with that song now." I am trying to teach her the consequences of interrupting.

She shrieks and begs me to sing again. I insist that she tell me whatever was so urgent she couldn't wait to share it between songs. We are cowboys facing off at high noon—a scene that repeats itself dozens of times in our house each day.

From mismatched white cribs on the opposite side of the room, her two-year-old brothers are tossing out song requests like drunks at a piano bar: "Rubber Duckie," "La La Lu," "How Much Is That Doggie in the Window?"

"All right, then," I say at last. "I'm going to sing Will's song for him, because he didn't interrupt." I am several lines into "Eidelweiss" when my daughter begins to choke out angry tears. Bewildered, I go and sit on the edge of the brass twin bed that was mine when I was her age.

"Honey, what is it?"

"Ma . . . ma . . . I . . . don't . . . think . . . you . . . love me." She hiccups out the words.

"What?" I am genuinely startled. "Why?"

"I don't . . . think . . . it's nice for you . . . to sing only . . . to Will!" She wails.

"Huh? But I . . . " Understanding dawns on me. "Oh, sweetie." I pull her close to me; frustration makes her small body tense and unwieldy. "I'm not singing only to Will. I'm singing to you and Mac too." I feel her body slacken. "I would never sing only to one of my children and leave the others out. But I can see why you thought that. That was my fault—I didn't explain myself very well at all." As I rock and hold her, hot tears baptize my chest and neck. She struggles to catch her breath, clinging to me. "I love you more than anything in the world," I tell her. "I would never hurt you on purpose. I'm *so* sorry."

Sooner than I expect, she is calm again, and I tuck her back into bed, in between salty kisses and more apologies. I move to leave, think better of it, turn back.

"Honey." I reach out to touch her cheek and she seizes my hand in both of hers. "I am so glad you told me what was going on, so we could fix it. You are really good at saying what you are feeling. I love that about you."

Eugenia sits up and hugs me again, hard. "Mama," she says. "Guess what? I love you. You're my sweet one, ever in the whole world."

This is my daughter.

I cannot believe my luck.

PASSING
IT ON

Zen Mind, Daughter's Mind

**GAYLE
BRANDEIS**

My daughter declared herself a Buddhist when she was eight. We were on a two-week road trip through the Southwest and were taking a fairly Zen approach to the whole thing; we had one destination in mind—our friends' wedding in Boulder—but otherwise, we had no itinerary, no reservations, no goals. We wanted to see where the road would take us, see where we would land each night. We ended up in some amazing places—Mesa Verde, Ghost Ranch, a parade in the middle of Santa Fe. One night, in Zion, Utah, Hannah was rifling through the drawers of our rustic hotel room. She found the usual stuff—some stationery, a local magazine, a phone book, the ubiquitous Gideon's Bible—but she also found a collection of Buddhist stories. The cover was a riot of color, much more appealing than Gideon's brown pleather offering. She brought it with her to her nest on the floor (she and her brother took turns sleeping on the second beds in our hotel rooms and camping on carpets). When she stood back up, she was a fully converted Buddha girl.

I have been a pseudo-Buddhist myself since my senior year of high school. A Pseuddhist, if you will. My journey started with a book too—I read Siddhartha, by Herman Hesse, a novel about the young Buddha on his path to enlightenment, and that was that. I loved how Siddhartha had to engage himself fully in the world—through sex and love, plus less enticing things, like poverty and pain—before he found Nirvana. I picked up other books, like Zen Mind, Beginners Mind, and loved learning about mindfulness—letting go of expectation, being here now, being open to life, each tiny moment of it. After years of hiding out in my own head, Buddhism helped me begin to feel much more present and whole inside my skin.

In college, I studied Buddhist art and history, performed with an experimental Buddhist theater group, and dabbled in meditation. (Although I never quite got the hang of zazen. Walking meditation was much more my speed. Slow, but in motion. I got much too antsy sitting still.)

For my study abroad my senior year, I chose to travel to Bali with a group from the Naropa Institute (now Naropa University), a Tibetan Buddhist–based college in Boulder, Colorado. One day, I went for a hike with the poet Anne Waldman near the temple at Goa Gaja. We came upon a statue of Buddha amongst some mossy stones; Bali is a Hindu island, so this was a bit of a surprise. Anne immediately dropped to her knees and touched her forehead to the ground.

"All disciples of Buddha need to genuflect at his image," she said. I could feel her waiting for me to fall to my knees too.

I wanted to be a good girl, a good Buddhist. I admired (and still admire) Anne so deeply—I had done an oral report about her in a poetry class just a month before I found out I was going to be traveling with her—but I couldn't bring myself to genuflect. I wasn't a disciple. I told myself that Buddha would like the fact that I didn't bow before him—

didn't he say "If you meet the Buddha in the road, kill him"?—but I still felt a bit like a failure. We spent the rest of the hike in silence—companionable silence, but a silence I managed to fill with doubt. A few days later, I found out I was pregnant, and any sense of Buddhist detachment I might have developed over the previous few years flew right out the window.

Since then, I've tried to incorporate Zen stuff into my parenting—being present and compassionate and mindful with my kids (not that I am always successful at it). Until Hannah expressed interest in Buddhism though, I had never really shared my Buddhist leanings with them. Maybe because I felt I was never fully "getting it"—I was just a dabbler, a dilettante in the Buddhist world. Especially when it came to letting go of attachment, which I think is the hardest precept to follow as a parent. Parenting is all about attachment. (Especially attachment parenting, which I practiced to a fault when my kids were little. Their bodies were glommed onto mine pretty much 24/7.)

I became very excited when Hannah "converted." I could finally share this Eastern-leaning part of myself with her. We could talk about these ideas together. Maybe we could even take a stab at the dreaded zazen. But she wasn't interested in sharing her Buddhism with me. It was her thing, and her thing alone.

One of my friends gave Hannah a little Buddha-in-a-box kit. It came with a small statue of Buddha, a booklet about Buddhism and meditation, and some incense and a stand to set it in. Hannah spent a lot of time poring over the booklet and attempting meditation in her room, with the door closed. She wasn't allowed to light the incense without supervision, but that was the only part of the process I was allowed to be part of. The rest was between Hannah and the Buddha. I suppose the whole situation should have made me a better Pseuddhist—it *was* a real exercise in letting go of expectation—but mostly, it made me feel sad. Hannah and I were alike in so many ways, and I was hoping Buddhism could make us even closer. But we also had a common pull toward doing things on our own, in our own way, and I had to respect that.

Buddhism often became more a source of contention between us than a source of connection. If Hannah started to whine when I wouldn't buy her some toy at the store or let her have a piece of candy before dinner, I would say "That's not very Buddhist of you," and she would glower at me as if I had just told her she was evil incarnate. I would proceed to lecture her about how the second noble truth of Buddhism states that all suffering is caused by desire. If she didn't want things so badly, she wouldn't end up being so upset. This never went over well. It often ended, in fact, with Hannah screaming "Then I don't want to be Buddhist anymore!" But she always went back to calling herself Buddhist (and sometimes Jewddhist, when she was feeling connected to our Jewish heritage). And I kept realizing how much desire I had to transcend, myself. The desire to shape my daughter into a smaller version of myself, the desire to share the exact same path with her. I needed to learn how to be fully present with her as she was, and let go of how I wanted her, wanted us, to be.

Hannah is eleven now. She doesn't identify herself as a Buddhist as readily these days, although she still thinks Buddhism is "cool." When I asked her what she liked about it, she said, "The serenity. And it's not against other religions. And it's in harmony with nature. And it's Japanese." Hannah's obsession with Buddhism has translated into an obsession with Japan. She loves everything about Japanese culture—the food, the music, the festivals, the aesthetic. Her room is a shrine to Japan, filled with paper lanterns and calligraphy scrolls and miniature plastic food. She collects manga graphic novels and is filling notebooks with her own wide-eyed characters. She is learning karate. She is teaching herself to read kanji. She even convinced me to dye her hair black. She is not Jewddhist now so much as Jewpanese. She is fully her own person, on her own unique journey. I think it's easier for me to see this, to honor this, when our obsessions take us in different directions. And as my girl grows bigger, grows away from me, as I learn to let go bit by bit, my heart clenches, then opens, like a lotus in my chest.

Twenty Minutes

JILL
SILER

My youngest daughter, Dezi, just turned eighteen. She's graduating from high school in a few months. She's petite, soft spoken, and flutters around as if she's weightless. She's leaving for college in September. I am lucky enough to give her a ride to school this morning because her boyfriend's car is broken. I wish it would stay broken until she's twenty, or at least until she's gone. She comes downstairs pulling on a bright green T-shirt with bold black letters across the front that spell out AGAINST ME. It makes her pale skin seem translucent, her hazel eyes green, and her inky black hair even more dramatic.

We sip tea before we leave and chat about college housing in Gainesville. Suddenly she begins to talk about how moved she is by Professor McGonagall's devotion to Dumbledore. She loves Harry Potter, Shakespeare, and recently Kerouac. On the short drive across the beach, she opens her window, looks away, and furtively takes a few puffs off a cigarette, hating to smoke in front of me but needing to. I don't point out that she's a vegetarian, for God's sake; honor the temple! I don't say a word about how her IQ is high enough to boil water, so she must know how many hateful toxins she is inviting into her perfect body. I don't rant and rave about all the people that will die today—a dozen in the next five minutes!—because they thought they were immune to the slim white stick she's sucking on right now. She throws the butt out the window and offers me her cockeyed, Mona Lisa smile. For just a pinch of a second, I am catapulted back through time. I feel the weight of her body in my arms and see her head lifting from my breast between huge gulps, her eyes glazed from the bliss of warm milk, and then her baby mouth smiling that same smile.

I ask her what she's looking forward to today. She says getting out of school early. She brushes some stray hairs away from her eyes, and I can't help but stare at the bright pink skin on either side of the industrial bar that's jabbed through the top of her left ear; once you're eighteen, you can get pierced anywhere with anything—legally. Impulsively and quick as a breath, I touch the very top of her ear with just the bare tip of my finger, wishing, wishing, wishing, sending, sending, sending healing energy to the inflamed area. I pretend to adjust a few wisps of hair she might have missed.

Across the street from her school, we pull up onto the grassy area where I drop her off. She leans forward, puts her right foot on the dashboard and tightens the Kermit shoelace on her green, Converse All Star sneaker. She calls them "chucks." They're still in pretty good shape. I run my thumb across her back, offering a silent blessing before she leaves. She flings open the door and looks over her shoulder to say goodbye. I want to keep her with me longer than the twenty minutes of this morning commute. I want to say, "Hey, honey, I have an idea! Let's just go hang out. We could go to the movies or hit the Hialeah thrift shops." But I know she has to go to school. I know she cuts too much as it is with her boyfriend, Felipe. I put my window down though, just in case; maybe there's a word or two left to say.

"Sure I can't just stay home today?" she asks before closing the door. "Mr. Bowman's absent. We could do . . . something. . . . " She taunts me; both of us know I would rather spend time with her than almost anyone on earth. I wiggle my fingers, waving goodbye. "Bye, Mom," she says. Then the smile.

"Bye, honey. Have a good day," I call after her. "Love ya, sweetheart." She takes a few steps toward the street and looks back at me again.

Today I get an "I love you too, Mom."

She walks toward Miami Beach High School, making her way across the street. A woman honks at her to hurry up and I resist the overwhelming urge to jump out of my car and smash the villain's head into her windshield. Dezi is oblivious, already lost in the day ahead of her. I watch her adjust her backpack, and I curse the weight of those books. I see her step onto the questionable safety of school property, black pigtails bouncing, her green T-shirt brilliant in the Miami sunshine. I think of flowers blooming around her. She's almost to the school doors now. It's a wretched school, I think again. I've always hated the wire fences and penitentiary ambience.

I want to do it all over again. I want to raise her in the country and let her go to a school that feels like a sanctuary. I should have stayed in Indiana. I should have kept her in St. Pat's. I should take her to the mountains in North Carolina while there's still time. I press my fingers against my eyelids, and rest my forehead on the steering wheel. I hate myself. What kind of woman would raise her daughters on Miami Beach?

I sit up and look through the window. Dezi turns her head, and I think I might be busted, so I start messing with the mirror. But instead she looks at someone calling her name. The faded aqua metal doors of the school open wide, and hundreds of students swarm through. She tugs at her backpack again and disappears into the rush. The last stragglers trail in, and the wind kicks up, moving turbulent, unpredictable clouds across the sky. I want to reach up and hold them still for a minute. Dezi's presence, like a fragrance, lingers everywhere as I drive away.

Isolation

BARBARA CARD ATKINSON

When I first became pregnant, I reverently wished for a boy.

It wasn't that I didn't want a girl, or that I had some notion that a boy would be "better." It was because of my mother. Such a cliché, but it does always seem to be about one's mother, doesn't it? Throughout much of my adolescence, my mother and I had clashed in horrific, drawn-out, passive-aggressive power plays, her wishes for me ferociously knotted up into the unfulfilled wants she had for herself. I felt consumed by what seemed to be her desire to mold me into an image she had of me, of herself, of us.

If I had a boy, there would be an obvious demarcation between myself and my child; boundaries would be excruciatingly clear. With a boy, I could learn how to mother someone entirely separate from myself. A girl would come later, I thought, when I was a seasoned pro. Being any less prepared seemed terrifying.

The baby was, of course, a girl.

And of course—because, like the mother cliché, that's how these things go—the very moment she was revealed as a she, I fell in love with her.

No, that's wrong. "Falling in love" describes an emotion in its infancy, a burgeoning state. Before I even met her, when what I saw of her was little more than a ghostly foot unveiled in the darkness of a sonogram screen, I felt something far beyond the act of moving into the state of love.

Think of the earth: a nice planet, has its difficulties, but it means well. Right? Sustainable unto its own system and all that? The earth is what I was before motherhood, a planet moving through space and time, clueless. And then I turned and saw a whole solar system, saw that I was just one part of a huge and gorgeous and complex universe.

She did that to me: Hannah.

When Hannah was just an infant, my husband and I had to relocate from a cheerful, suburban apartment with a nearby playground to a rental home at the edge of an industrial complex. I had already been feeling the indigenous isolation of new motherhood, with no family nearby to offer advice or simply to hold the baby while I showered. Suddenly I found myself even more cut off, living on a gravel-strewn street with no other residents (much less a cadre of sympathetic mothers) nearby, and my husband was working longer hours than ever. The move was a physical manifestation of what I felt internally: I was alone with this baby. Alone. No man is an island, but every new mother is a sandbar, with regular tidal flooding and the occasional threat of submersion.

Although I was desperately lonely and often exhausted by the concept and execution of venturing far from our tiny, marooned home in order to see my friends, there was also a simple sweetness to our quiet life. It was akin to living on a homestead—if your average homestead had gravel trucks grinding gears just past the front lawn and catering companies spewing grease fumes across the backyard fence. I knew that during the day there would be no interruptions—no neighbors dropping by, no salespeople knocking, no outside world inviting itself over for tea. Hannah and I were alone. We walked a great deal; first with her in the carrier or stroller, and eventually with her walking alongside me (such slow, slow walks), discussing the social lives of her imaginary friends. Sometimes it was reading a book while she napped, her head heavy against me, and later making dinner while she perched on a kitchen chair over the sink, washing her tea-set dishes as we made up songs.

Years later, I still marvel that I survived the claustrophobia of that time, marked by maternal exhaustion, a high-intensity toddler, and an ancient dog rattling around a tiny house, surrounded by the tundra of an ice-slicked yard. I don't miss it. What I do miss now that Hannah is older is that sense of being more in my daughter's world—being, in some ways, my daughter's whole world.

Hannah's a tween now, and I feel more often than not at the periphery of her life. She has friends, she has hobbies, and she shows an appalling lack of both ability and interest when it comes to dishing the details of her inner life. I often cannot even get her to tell me when she last ate, much less what it was. To be the mother of a preteen daughter is a whole new kind of isolation.

There's an old saying: The two worst years in a woman's life are the year she is thirteen and the year her daughter is. When I was thirteen, my mother was a cipher to me, but no more so than I was a cipher to myself. She was shifting, in my eyes, from Omniscient Mother to Simpering Wife, even as I was fighting my own violent surges between Shy Young Woman and Independent Siren. With every move my mother made to reconnect, I would rail. If she absentmindedly stroked my hair as I passed, there would be a sudden vacuum only I could feel sucking all the oxygen out of the room. A sideways glance at my carefully chosen outfit, my book, my friends, and I would stomp out of the room, exhausted by her unspoken critique. Is that the unstable ground to which we are traveling, Hannah and I, a place of unspoken recriminations and bitter disappointments? Will I soon be desperately chasing this child who for so long fiercely clung to me? How could my mother not stroke me as I passed, when I myself touch and kiss and sniff my children as automatically as breathing? The urge to hold them, pet them, is visceral and unrelenting.

Does it fade, or will I be a wizened old woman, hunched awkwardly as I attempt to blow raspberries against the belly of my exasperated, restrained fifty-year-old?

I did have that son I wished for, five years after the birth of my daughter. The worries with him were all about how to take care of two children, when learning how to care for the first one had knocked me so cleanly to my knees. He's a miniature Borscht Belt comedian, all for the spontaneous dropping of trou and a good potty joke. I don't worry that we'll have to work to rediscover each other the way Hannah and I might. He loves me the way all the clichés said he would, like a fickle lover. He sprays kisses up and down my arms before I leave for work, for a walk, to pick up the mail—and then he turns away and forgets me entirely until I return. As he hits his tweens, it won't be me he'll see when he looks in the mirror. I can't imagine that he'll need to separate from me as much when we are so clearly separate now. He feels it, or why would he chase me so?

The image of me lurks within my daughter, in how her breasts will bud and how the shadows will hit the curve of her cheek, in how she suspects she will grow into whom she does and does not want to become. It's her job to knock down the fences I erected simply by being here before her, and it's my job to repair them the best I can.

Hannah's attention is now often diverted by the latest online game, by a book or a phone call, her lankiness draped across a chair at a vertebra-cracking angle. I want her to blossom and to stretch and to do all of those other things that are metaphors for independence, don't get me wrong. I enjoy no longer having to do my manic Ms. Frizzle voice or having to grimly push her imaginary friend on a swing (as she strictly instructed me to do while she went to chase butterflies nearby and left me to push and sing, push and sing to an empty swing while other mothers in the park eyed me warily). But—oh!—where is that sticky hand wrapped around my finger, those feet stumbling slightly as we inch our way around the block, stopping to look at every rock and flower and bug? Where is the weight of that buttery-scented, sleeping head on my shoulder? It's funny that I ever worried she would not feel separate from me when I find myself so carefully, delicately trying to rewrap those tender threads that connected us.

Time Capsule

**JODY
MACE**

Today I wrote a letter, a love letter of sorts, to a young woman whom I haven't met yet. She is my daughter, Kyla.

Kyla is nine, and it was her idea to make a time capsule for herself, to be opened in four years, when she's thirteen. She thought it would be fun when she's a teenager to look back at herself at age nine. She said that her memory of being nine might be "fuzzy," like her memory of being five is now. My first thought was that she was missing the point of time capsules. Time capsules are to be sealed for a long period of time, fifty or a hundred years, in order to tell the people of the future what life was like in the past. You don't make a time capsule for just four years.

But when I saw the objects that she was putting in the box, I started to think again. There was a picture of her beloved guinea pigs, Butterball and Slinky, and a small toy horse with a soft mane. She included a bag of horse chestnuts—called "conkers" by English children and used for games—that she gathered when we lived in England last year. There was also a bookmark that she had made and a noisemaker that had been a featured instrument in the cacophonic parades that she and her brother staged around the house. (I wasn't sorry to see that go.)

She put these objects into the decorated shoebox with no sentimentality, but I was struck by how they were all tokens from her girlhood. At nine, she loves her pets (quite possibly more than she loves her younger brother) and is in heaven when she gets the rare chance to ride a horse. I imagine an archaeologist examining these artifacts, putting them together to construct a picture of their owner: a girl who adores animals, reads voraciously, hoards things from nature, and is still young enough to love making noise for the sheer joy of it.

In four years, where will that girl be? There is a great chasm between a nine-year-old and a thirteen-year-old. It might as well be a hundred years.

Kyla wrote a letter to herself for the time capsule. It is a breezy letter, with fancy, purple letters. "Dear Me," she writes, and lists the things she likes: guinea pigs, puppies, the movie Shrek. She signs it with a flourish: "I hope you like this, Kyla! Love, Me," her signature girlishly surrounded by hearts. I'm struck by the un-self-conscious, childlike nature of her letter. She seems unaware that she's at the brink of a great change in her life.

But I'm aware. And so when she decides she'd like letters from me and other relatives to go into her time capsule, I am rendered temporarily wordless by the responsibility of saying something to this daughter that I don't know yet. I know my nine-year-old Kyla as well as a mother can know a daughter, but this Kyla of the future is a stranger to me. What will she like doing? Will she roll her eyes when I give her my words of wisdom? Will she have turned "boy crazy"? Will she be earnest like she is now, or will the chaotic assault of puberty have turned her into a cynic?

Other parents I know have noticed their self-assured daughters losing confidence as they entered adolescence. Often these girls stopped speaking up in class, started thinking they were dumb at math; some even decided that it benefited their popularity to get bad grades. What can I write to thirteen-year-old Kyla to inoculate her against these dangers?

Sometimes I'm scared about Kyla's not-too-distant entry into adolescence. Even now I sense the prepubescent rumblings. She sometimes says that she is confused but can't quite put into words what is confusing her. She has started to pay increased attention to her appearance. Sure, she still frequently paints her face to look like a tiger, but she can also spend twenty minutes putting her hair into a stylish bun with bobby pins. At times, a seemingly minor incident brings her to tears, and she is bewildered by her own emotional eruptions. I wonder if hormones are beginning to make their appearance.

So I struggle for words for my letter. I want to give her advice that will steel her against the dog-eat-dog world that middle-school girls often inhabit. Something like Rudyard Kipling's "If," only adapted for the seventh-grader: "If you can keep your head when your best friend tells you that she's not your friend anymore and that she's having a sleepover with all her friends and you're not invited; if you can believe in yourself when the girl who sits next to you in math class hisses that your shirt is *so* last year, and, being gossiped about, you do not gossip, then you'll be a woman, my daughter!" But the words fall flat. I have the feeling that there is no advice that will guard her heart against cruelty.

And honestly, advice doesn't even go over that well with her now. Kyla likes to figure things out for herself. I can't imagine that she will be excited about reading a letter full of advice from me when she's thirteen. Finally it strikes me that the best person to influence Kyla is Kyla. I decide to paint a picture of the self-assured girl she is now and just hope that that girl will reach four years into the future to give her vulnerable older self a boost of the confidence that she has now.

I start with silly details to jog her memory: "You like to sleep late and to wear your green monkey pajamas. Your favorite foods are Cocoa Pebbles, macaroni and cheese, and pizza." I want her to get a glimpse of her younger self. "You love to play piano and to hold your guinea pigs and to draw."

I remind her of her strengths, just in case she's forgotten. Kyla is a peacemaker during schoolyard conflicts, treating everyone as her friend. "I wonder if you know how special you are. You are one of the kindest, most loving people I've ever known. You include all your friends and try to never make anyone feel hurt." I write about her talents at school, including writing and math, and how she seeks out challenging work, not giving up until her intellectual curiosity is satisfied. Finally, I tell her that she can always come to me to talk, and that I love her.

The letter feels inadequate, but it's the best I can do. I'm just one voice, and even though I'm her mother, I wonder how much help my one voice will offer when there are so many discouraging voices around her— the voices of peers who will sometimes tear her down, the voices from popular culture that tell her that her worth is measured by her appearance, and her own inner voice, which may at times be more doubting than empowering. Then I remember about the other letters that she requested.

I ask her dad, her grandfather, aunts, and uncles to write letters. Teachers and other adult friends get the request as well. Maybe none of us knows quite the right thing to say. But I hope that the sheer volume of caring words will drown out any negative words that she might be hearing. The letters start coming in: "To be opened by Kyla in 2008." All the letters, sealed, go into her time capsule to stay unopened until she is thirteen. And then she will be greeted into young womanhood with a chorus of love from people who will be telling her, "You are special. We love you. Welcome!"

I think a lot about the girl who will open that box. Everyone who wrote a letter to her probably has a different vision of who she will become. I'm in no better position than anyone else to hazard a guess. She has always surprised me. Sometimes—when she gets lost listening to music or runs to check her email, or when I notice her legs seeming to lengthen overnight—I get a glimpse of the future, and I can imagine, just for a moment, what a thirteen-year-old Kyla might be like. But then she does something completely childlike—she skips instead of walks, or asks me to count how many bounces she can do on the pogo stick—and she's nine again, her adolescence years away. So we wait. And while she waits to see what is in the time capsule, I wait and watch, little by little, the mystery of my daughter unfold.

The Boy We Didn't Have

KATHERINE WEBER

I adore my two daughters, and I adore being the mother of daughters. I don't mean that in the superficial sense of, say, talking about eye make-up or trying on clothing together—in fact, I am pretty deficient when it comes to being that kind of mother to daughters. What I mean is, before I had any actual reason to know who they were, before they were born, I somehow felt their femaleness, and I felt an incredible "girls together" bond with each of them from the first moments I felt them moving inside me, when they were their earliest, swimmy, distinctive, embryonic selves. We were like nesting cups, the inevitable little girl body inside my bigger girl body both times.

By the time they were born, I felt as if I had already come to know both Lucy and Charlotte in some intangible ways that left my husband out entirely. In each pregnancy, I had the advantage of months of those afternoon, drowsy/queasy biology-is-destiny-after-all naps, during which I communed with the hiccupping, tumbling, kicking presence occupying and preoccupying me. Both times, as the pregnancy advanced and I got larger, the pregnancy inhabiting every part of my body, I felt intriguingly primitive, like a broody mama cave woman. *Me big woman. Me have baby. You, man, go fetch food so me can be strong to have baby. Give me meat! Also spaghetti, and don't forget marinara sauce!*

I also felt philosophical during my pregnancies, in a dopey way, prone to profound insights such as, *Oh my god! This is where people come from.*

It was certainly where my daughters came from, and it was, in fact, a truly profound experience to deliver them both into the world, with my husband talking me through it. I had never felt more female in my life than I did pushing those babies out of my body and into the world in two wonderful, intense, unmedicated deliveries. I was strong and determined, but also, I had the good luck to possess the right pelvic bones.

Although Lucy's gender was unknown right until the delivery—and even then, one of the delivery nurses saw the thatch of dark hair on the top of her head as it crowned and declared, "I'm getting boy vibes!"—she emerged as the girl I knew she would be, just as her sister Charlotte would a year and a half later. That time, an ultrasound technician had tipped us off, but it was no surprise. If we had gone on to have another, or two more, or even three more children, I am utterly certain they would have all been girls. For no logical reason, I believe I am designed to have girls, wired to be the mother of girls.

It's not that I think boys have cooties. (Although, I have to say, the few times I have ever changed a baby boy's seriously used diaper—a complex industrial procedure requiring a great deal of intimate manipulation—it made me consider in new ways the origins of certain male expectations that women be eager and admiring handlers of the goods.) It's just that I can hardly imagine what it would have been like to have one of my own, to have raised one, day in, day out.

It's different for my husband. I think he has always been able to imagine it well. He was once a little boy, after all, so he knows more about what we're missing, while my own experience of growing up has always connected me in all sorts of ways to our daughters at every stage. But there are times when I admit that I do miss the boy we didn't have. Sure, the boy who would have played with trains and cars, the Little Leaguer, he would have been fun to have around. (Though who's to say what kind of boy he would have been?) Yes, I know my husband has long had a particularly wistful experience passing by the little sport jackets at Brooks Brothers. He would have loved to teach a son to hit a cross-court backhand, he would have loved to have a son to take on a hike, a son with whom to play squash on Saturday mornings and eat rice pudding at a diner afterward, the way he and his own father spent Saturday mornings long ago. But the boy we didn't have, the ghost of that boy—he's most missed, I think, by me, when my husband and daughters are immersed in their father–daughter intensities and I feel like the wallflower at the dance, the one without a date, the one who watches all the other couples having a great time.

Does it seem odd to wish to add a cross-current to the ongoing oedipal family drama, for balance? The inevitable attractions and loyalties and intensities that connect a father and his daughters—and there has never been a more intensely devoted father to his daughters than Nick—could be nicely balanced by something flowing the other way at times, and that's when I speculate about that unique bond connecting a boy and his mother. Yes, my daughters and I are close. And my husband and I are close too. And sisterhood is powerful. But the three of them have the opposite-gender parent–child layer of connection, and at certain times I am the odd man out. What am I missing exactly? I will never really know.

A friend of mine, the mother of two boys, told me that she was once chatting with a friend about having two boys and no daughters, and that she said to her friend offhandedly, "After Jeffrey was born, sometimes we thought about having another child. A girl would have been nice."

She didn't know that Jeffrey, age nine, was eavesdropping on the conversation, which traumatized him for days until he tearfully told her what he had heard and she could reassure him. Because he had taken her to mean, in that overly literal fashion of children, that his parents sometimes wished for *another child*, a different child, a girl child instead of him, the second boy.

Our daughters are in their twenties now, and our family has long felt complete. We never really considered another child, and we certainly never wished for *another child*. I write novels with male characters whose names are among those we once considered long ago. But every now and then, there is a moment. I hear Nick's voice light up a certain way when he answers the phone, and it is Lucy or Charlotte calling. Sometimes I'm the one who answers the phone, and one of our daughters will chat with me before asking, in a certain way—"Is Daddy there?" And I feel it, just for an instant, that little void, the space in our family occupied by nothing, the ghost of the boy we didn't have.

Learning to Write

**ANDREA J.
BUCHANAN**

Emi is ambivalent.

She is five years old, losing her baby fat and gaining the responsibilities of a kindergartner. At school she loves the thrill of being in "K," though she is anxious over the newness of it all. At home, she revels in her status as an older sibling even as she is bitterly jealous about having to share me with her brother. Some days she wants to play "new baby," where I have to tend to her while she wails and moans the way she never did as an infant; other days she gets into my makeup, stuffs her favorite Panda down her shirt to make Panda boobies, and tells me, "Look, I'm a grownup!" She alternates between clingy "I love you"s and petulant shouts to leave her alone. She tells me one night that she dreamt about being alone in the deep end of a big swimming pool without her floaties, that she almost drowned.

I bear the brunt of her ambivalence. I am the one she desperately demands, the one she snappishly pushes away. I am told this is the hallmark of the mother–daughter relationship, this constant push–pull, but that does little to reassure me.

There was a moment after she was born, when she was so small and I was so fragile—newly delivered of a baby, newly made a mother—when I held all six pounds of her sleeping in my arms and felt a shock of recognition. This little baby in my arms was me; I was my grownup self, holding my baby self. My god, I thought, we have completely merged. And yet as soon as I felt that realization spread over my body like the warm rush of alcohol, I knew that as much as she was me, she was also not-me, that even when she was inside me, she was herself, her own person. I was awed by this intense, ambivalent closeness we shared, and by the simultaneous and eternal separation between us.

And now I worry, as she grows older and these stages of connection and distance ebb and flow, that the separation might win out.

Emi began to write her name shortly before she turned three. Soon after, she recognized it everywhere, finding "E"s and "M"s and "I"s on signs, in magazines, on my computer keyboard. At three and a half, she added "Mommy" and "love" to the repertory of words she could write, and almost every drawing I have saved from when she was that age has "Mommy," "Emi," and "love" written somewhere on it. Words, in those early days, were like pictures for her: She drew letters as though she was designing fonts—adding flourishes and shadows, writing everything entirely in outline, or putting curlicues on the end of each letter and hearts over her lowercase "i"s like a junior-high girl in love. She copied letters from magazines or boxes or book covers and reproduced them exactly as she saw them, only tangentially interested in the idea that these letter-pictures made sense in a way other than the purely visual.

When Emi begins kindergarten, I'm confident that she will shine in the classroom, what with her excellent artistic skills and penchant for fanciful serifs. But as I stay close during the morning drop off, helping her get settled into her "journal work," I note her tendency each day to draw a version of the same picture—herself with family members and friends—and next to that, the same list, every day, of all the words she knows how to write without help. This seems to be reassuring to her, the ease of repetition, the familiarity of drawing people and words she already knows.

At our first kindergarten parent–teacher conference, the teachers comment on her reluctance to stray outside her comfort zone. She continues to write that roster of words each day, and she can write anything someone else can help her figure out how to spell, but when faced with a word she cannot picture in her head and cannot turn to someone else for help with, she is frustrated. It takes her too long. She gives up. The teachers suggest I encourage her to try new things, to spell words even if they come out "wrong," to try to help her connect the concept of the way a letter looks with the sound it makes.

They show me her journal: lots of family pictures, that same list of words and names. November 2, 2004, reads: "I love you, John Kerry," five words she knows how to spell on her own.

At home, after the conference, when Emi asks me to help her spell words, I try to encourage her to sound things out and write down the letters she hears. But she is too frustrated. "Just let me do it my way!" she yells, drawing wavy lines of pretend cursive as she narrates a story about a mommy who never lets a daughter do things her own way.

She huffs off and returns in a few moments with a small rectangular pad of paper, scribbling things down and ripping off sheets as if she is handing out traffic tickets. She places the papers in various locations, and

I come over to see what she's done. I'm expecting to see a love letter, her usual "I LOVE YOU MOMMy" or "EMi LOVES MOMMy."

But next to the cat is a paper that says, "NO CAT."

Next to her sleeping baby brother is a paper that says, "NO NATE."

She thrusts a paper in my hand, and it says, "NO MOMMy."

She sticks a paper on herself that immediately drops to the floor. It says, "NO EMi."

"What is this, Em?" I ask.

"Stop it!" she says. "I'm making a trail!"

She writes an arrow on her pad of paper, tears off the sheet, and places it on the floor. She draws another arrow on another paper and places it next to the first arrow. She repeats the process until she has covered the kitchen floor in a paper path of arrows pointing in various directions.

"You have to follow the map," she commands me, so I do. I step into the kitchen and follow the arrows one by one until I arrive at the last paper. I can see the expression on Emi's face is one of peevish delight. She knows I will not like what I'm about to see.

It says "No MOMMy No LOVE," and it has a heart that has been crossed out with a big X. I hold the paper, which might as well be a knife in my gut, and then she says, "Look on the back."

It says, "No LOVE MOMMy."

These are all words she knows, all words she can spell by herself, arranged in a way I haven't seen from her before. I catch her eye and I can see her trying to gauge my expression. She looks triumphant but also worried. I try to keep my face neutral, though I know it always betrays me. But then she is already an expert reader of my emotions. She knows she has hit her mark.

"Oh," I say. "That really hurts my feelings."

Immediately, I realize I have made a mistake. She is not three—she is not trying out the power of words, seeing how far she can go or determining exactly what is acceptable. She is not asking for a lesson about the difference between friendly words and hurtful words. She is five now. She isn't testing me: She's trying to communicate with me.

As I pick up the arrow-marked papers from the floor, my initial hurt gives way to the realization that my work as a mother with Emi is not to be liked by her, but to love her. I am supposed to be her safe place—the one person to whom she can vent, who she knows for sure will not leave. My obvious deflation upon reading her message—my fallen face and my focus on my own hurt feelings—has called this safety into question, making her consider a whole other realm of possibility. Does she have the power to hurt me? Will this power make me leave? Is her anger something she needs to protect me from? She seems both smug and scared by the prospect.

I let her stomp off to write more impassioned missives, and when she comes back, her lip thrust out and pad in hand, I try to be nonchalant.

"You know what, Em? Actually, it's okay with me if you want to write down how you feel, and it's okay if you need to write something that might hurt my feelings. I love you, no matter what you need to write down. I just love you. No matter what."

I am trying to give her permission to be angry at me, to defy me with the written word. I am trying to remind myself that her assertion of herself does not mean a forever rejection of me. I am trying to remind us both that love is not a currency that depends on the exchange around it.

She confronts me with a stubborn frown and thrusts another small rectangle of paper in front of me. On it she has written: "I_DT_LiKE_YoU."

She reads it to me, her still-chubby index finger underlining each word as she pronounces it. "I. Don't. Like. You."

Last year at this time, when she was four, she told me she was writing a book. When I asked her what it was called, she said, "Emi Mommy Love." Now her topic seems to have mutated from a glowing fluff piece to a tell-all, and she is so motivated by her passion for the subject she has had to resort to using words she doesn't already know how to spell.

Her kindergarten teachers would be proud.

When she told me about her dream of being in the deep end of the pool with no floaties, I'd had to remind her that she knew how to swim. I reminded her that even if she forgot that she knew how to swim, she had learned how to float at summer camp, and that even if she didn't have arm floaties or a noodle with her, she could float herself right over to the edge of the pool, where she would be safe. She told me weeks after that first dream that she had another dream: She was way out deep in the ocean this time. She was there with her friends, and they couldn't swim, but this time they all floated with noodles.

This note to me is her attempt at swimming in deep waters.

Reading it, I am sobered a little as a mother, even as I am proud of her as a writer. This is what compelling writing is, after all—the powerful, authentic expression of a truth that needs to be stated, no matter how provocative it may be.

"Wow, Em," I say, struggling to keep my own face upbeat and smiling as I watch her expression flicker somewhere between mischievous disobedience and worry. "Look at this, you wrote 'don't,' even though you didn't know how to spell it! I'm proud of you!"

She screws up her face into a pout again, her expectations thwarted by my positive reaction, and yanks the paper from me before she walks away.

I can see the rest of her pad is filled with the usual "MOMMy DADDy Emi NATE CAT I LOVE YOU MOMMy LOVE Emi" writing she does so well. As my eyes sting, I think, *This is important, what we're doing here right now.* She needs to do this, and I need to let her. She is no longer that me/not-me baby in my arms.

"I_DT_LiKE_YoU" is a breakthrough, though she doesn't realize it. She has made a connection between the sound of a word and its physical representation. She has written words she did not know how to spell, and she has shown them to me even though she fears I will disapprove. But more than a breakthrough, it is a break, her first true break from her intense attachment to me. She has asserted herself as her own person with her own perspective on our relationship, and I must allow her this. I must be proud of her, no matter what message she has spelled out.

Passing It On

LESLIE LEYLAND
FIELDS

I stand in the stern of the skiff, and Naphtali is in the bow.

"Mom, could I run the skiff for the rest of the pick?"

"Sure," I reply instantly, my internal eyebrows rising. Finally, it's happening. "Wanna take it now?" I shout over the engine, careful to keep my face neutral. We are heading to the next net, the bow plunging between waves. She nods her head yes and makes her way back between the totes and skiff sides.

Naphtali, fourteen, now stands in my place in the stern; I move to the center of the skiff. She has gone out commercial salmon fishing with her father every day of every summer since she was nine, but she has resisted this move to the stern. Running the sixty-horse outboard means maneuvering a twenty-six-foot aluminum skiff around fishing nets on the open ocean. It requires finesse, aggression, and strength.

She grips the outboard handle tentatively and uses her body as I do, as a stabilizer for her left arm. The men don't need to do this; they have enough body weight and mass to absorb the intense vibration and the force of propulsion. As we approach the next net, she slows.

We come in for the landing on the net, and I see we won't make it. The wind is pushing us over the line.

"Sorry!" she calls as she reverses.

"That's okay! Let's go again!" I reply, facing out to the water, not watching her, giving her room.

We approach again. She slows the engine, idles us close to the corks, and shifts into neutral for me to lean over the skiff side and lift the net out of the water, but we are still five feet short.

"S'okay. Let's go again. This time, reverse until you're parallel to the net and then approach," I suggest, watching her this time.

She tries this maneuver, but as we get closer and I direct—"Reverse now!"—she turns the motor the wrong way, and we slide away from the net.

"Arrgggh! Which way do you turn this for reverse, Mom?"

"The other way. Turn it the other way!" She turns the arm sharply toward herself, but we turn the wrong direction.

Again we miss. Just feet short, the wind blusters the bow over the other side of the corks.

"Mom, maybe you should do it!" Naphtali calls, frustrated.

"No. You can do it." I will not tell her again how to do this, I decide. This is knowledge that comes not from language or shouted directives; it comes only through the hands, the shift of her feet. Her body must begin recording all the ways of moving a craft through the many waters she will face.

For me, this started when I was twenty, when I married a fisherman from Kodiak, Alaska, and stepped into this ancient, new world of salmon and fishing. That was twenty-eight years ago. I wasn't taught; I simply did it because I could, because my help was needed in the crush of fish, because the question of who I was—woman, girl, man, wife, fisherman—didn't matter then.

When we are done with our final net, Naphtali makes one more request: "Mom, can I take it to the tender?"

I smile casually, as if I don't know what this really means. "Sure, go ahead." She tightens her grip on the outboard handle, stands straighter, and rounds the corner of the island, face set in stoic confidence, the stern face her father wears, that her grandfather wore, that all the men wear as they command their vessel from the stern. The face I wear as well.

We head for the *Sierra Seas*, the larger boat that takes our fish and delivers it to the cannery. The other skiffs from our fishing operation are there—six of them, with two crewmen in each—all tied together, waiting to offload their fish. We see them before they see us. This is it—center stage. I glance up at Naphtali, her face still frozen with inscrutable aplomb. Then they hear us and glance in our direction. She is ready. This is her debut, her coming out. The Alaskan fishergirl's equivalent of a Southern girl's debutante ball. It's public now: Naphtali is running the skiff. Everyone sees and knows. She is no longer a child or a crewman or a girl; she is a fisherman.

What am I giving to you, daughter? I wondered that day. Though most of her training has been under her father's eye and hand, I am part of this too. What am I passing on to her? There is a sense of foreboding—perhaps what all parents feel as they begin to teach their teenagers to drive a car. You know that you are giving your child the means to grow up, get a job, be independent, but it is always so much more than that. You are giving them the keys to death, to accidents. In their two hands, for the first time, they will grip space and time on a wheel, and they will test what can be done in these dimensions.

Out here, the consequences are no less. Running a skiff makes you captain of a small ship, presiding over one or two crewmen. It means you earn the right to travel your piece of boat straight into a convulsed, tide-ripping storm of ocean and, in the midst of that storm, to fish and work as if there were none. It means you hold other people's lives in your hands. It means you work eight to fifteen hours every day of the week through every summer.

It means my daughter will be a girl in a world of men, and will be expected to work like a man, no matter her size. It means that just as she is becoming a woman, Naphtali is becoming a man.

I don't remember which day I became a woman on the water. But I became a man first.

It might have happened in a blow, when piloting a small skiff alone through fifty-knot winds. Or when the nets were so full of fish that we could not lift them from the water; we instead picked them in the water, throwing hundreds, thousands behind us into our skiffs for days, until we could no longer stand. Or on the night I drove a skiff full of fish around an island and a reef in the black dark, not knowing where the rocks were. Or the times I refused help from crewmen though I desperately needed it, my body near breaking. Or the nights we took up our nets—me, the smallest, choosing to pull the lead line, the heaviest line of all.

Then one day I became a woman again. Maybe it happened when I was out in the skiff with a baby ashore, my breasts filling with milk as the skiff filled with fish and I knew there was a helpless other who needed me more. Maybe it happened when I started accepting help, relying on my six-foot-two crewman who was twice my weight, choosing to preserve my back for all its other uses. Maybe it was when I looked beyond the fish to notice the crewman beside me, asking him how he was doing with this work. Maybe when I cried alone in the dark, running the skiff around the reef, praying for help, knowing then that anything I did was not done by my strength or any strength at all.

Growing up in New Hampshire, if I had thought about being a mother someday and passing a heritage onto my daughter, I would not have imagined this—the two of us out in a skiff, in orange raingear, slimed by fish guts, blood, and kelp, angling a skiff around a net, the mountains and ocean rising up around us. I would not have imagined us killing fish instead of garnishing them, snatching salmon from the ocean's jaws, shouting sea lions away from our nets, picking kelp at midnight, assessing people's worth by body size and strength.

Though I grew up in the '60s and '70s in a nearly genderless household—with three brothers and two sisters and a mother who built houses, fireplaces, and furniture—somehow, in a rosy glow, my vision of mothering a daughter places the two of us in the kitchen. There we are, within warm, buttery walls, surrounded by appliances with dashboards and buttons just waiting to be controlled by the lift of our fingers. Engines that whirr to life with a touch rather than a full-body yank on a six-foot pull cord. We wear matching aprons instead of matching raingear. I demonstrate the roll of the pin, the fold of the dough, instead of the slash of kelp and the roll of jellyfish from the nets. Betty Crocker is there; we speak of literature, *The Heart of Darkness, The God of Small Things*, as we braid a mound of challah. I teach her the science of yeasts and piecrusts, the brilliance of Indian curries. My daughter learns to savor the artistry of food as I do, the unending beauty of colors and textures and flavors—this, the only domestic art that I love.

None of this has happened. Naphtali, like her brothers, enters the kitchen only to eat. When I can leave my other labors—writing and the work of a house and children—I gear up, join her, and head out to sea.

Naphtali, now fifteen, and Noah, my oldest son, thirteen, are my crew tonight. Though they both run skiffs now, I'm taking my husband's place on the water and in the stern while he works ashore on the generator. It's a long run down to Seven-Mile Beach, where we start picking the nets. The water is troubled by a northeasterly wind, the sky grey. Noah sits quiet, head bobbing in the bounce of the waves, at peace with this work. Naphtali has a headache and closes her eyes the whole trip down. I think her period has started. She is tired and grumpy. This is their third pick of the day; they've already worked eight hours on the nets this morning and afternoon. I wonder what kind of mother I am. I want to send her home and to bed with an aspirin and hot chocolate instead of taking her back out to sea. I wish I were home myself. But this is our living. This is our work.

Halfway through the nets, she perks up, and between fish, we manage a small skirmishing dance, arm-waving steps on the fish-slippery floor of the skiff. We sing songs from *Fiddler on the Roof*, *My Fair Lady*, urgently redeeming the time, transcending the work and its slow, mind-numbing drag across our spirits. Noah does not sing with us. He does not need to.

Later, after delivering our fish to the tender, we find out the guys in the other skiffs called us "the cute skiff." Naphtali is angry to be singled out, to be seen as different from the men. Mostly, she is irritated to be seen as what she is: young, pretty, a girl—none of which has anything to do with her competence on the water. She wants only equality right now.

"Naphtali, be cute as long as you can," I advise her, knowing in my own body the tyranny of equity.

She glares at me.

"I'm tired of being around men all the time," Naphtali complains.

I go out with her on the next pick. She is sixteen now and takes her place automatically in the stern, which makes me her crew. Her face is deeply tanned from weeks out on the water; her cheeks are red, eyes a vivid green. I sit in front of her on the seat, partly protected by a chest-high plastic tote that holds our fish and ice. I feel small beneath her. She is taller and stronger than I am now. I gave up arm-wrestling her last year. Our catch so far is a paltry dozen-or-so red salmon, beautiful and rich to eat but hardly enough to pay for our gas this day. We have plenty of time to talk. We talk about the books we are reading. She has just finished Isabel Allende's *My Invented Country*. I tell her about *The Myth of the Perfect Mother* and J. M. Coetzee's *Disgrace*. We decide to trade books if the fishing stays slow.

Above us the mountains of the Alaskan peninsula hover like clouds over the water. The sun has warmed the wind to a gusty southwesterly twenty-five, just a day breeze, but enough to riffle the waters and peel their waves to white. Spray sluices us in regular, languid splats. A rogue wave suddenly hits us with fervor, a full face and shoulder wash for both of us. Naphtali turns her head and expertly hawks and spits a mouthful behind her. "I'm getting better at spitting," she announces. I nod my head, understanding.

She is the only female out on the water every day, at all hours. At sixteen, she trains and gives orders to new crewmen five to ten years older than her. I watch her as she works, how quickly she surveys the hang of the net, the position of the running line, the tidal currents, the wind. In an instant she knows what to do and tells me in clipped sentences what she expects of me. "Don't roller it—tide's too strong. Put the longer pole in the bow. Grab the running line." I comply, do all that she says. She is the expert now. No one would know we were mother and daughter. If anything, someone observing us from afar would reverse our identities, perhaps would even think: father and son.

When the nets are finished, we join our compatriots, the six other skiffs of brothers and hired crewman. Upon some signal invisible to me, all seven skiffs move from a lazy circling to a full-bore race to the tender. Naphtali leans forward, starting off in second place, bouncing over the top of the waves, then slicing through the troughs with that same mix of urgency and calm, while the other skiffs edge beside her. She wins, two minutes later raising her fist in the air, hooting in triumph as she sails into the anchorage. I sit beneath her, wondering, *How has this happened so quickly? And how much of this is my fault?*

Sixteen years ago I carried a newborn up the gravel path to the house we were still building. A house on a remote island in Alaska, with no running water, no plumbing. An island inhabited only by my husband, Duncan, and me—and now this baby. Until then, if anyone had asked me to describe the meaning of "helpless," I would have reached for a metaphor, "*Helpless*" is like. . . . But that day, I held the meaning itself in my arms, the word incarnated in the flesh of this being. And in service to her, I gave myself over: I was her food, her arms, her legs, her sleep. My body was hers, my mind, my heart—all hers.

Several times a day I would lay her on her stomach. She would strain to lift her head a few inches to gawk about, holding her bobbing gaze as long as she could, then collapse into a wail of frustration. I would let her cry for a minute, then move her on to the next "station"—an infant seat, where she would bounce contently for three minutes, gaping at the gallery of cutout magazine faces, until the next cry and the move to the next station, on the floor above the Sesame Street gym. The rotations were interrupted only by nursings, walks on the hillside (where I could watch the men out on the nets, my former life), whatever other diversion I could devise.

By the fourth week of motherhood, both my concept and practice of strength had changed utterly. Competence and muscle were no match against this baby. I began to glimpse then the long slow courage needed to simply persevere through the days, years, minutes of patient attendance she required. Time felt like the enemy, the ever-lengthening barrier between this helpless infant and who I hoped she would become someday: an upright, articulate, fully capable being.

Through these long hours alone—with Duncan out fishing and no roads, no escape from the house and the island, no contact with the outside world—I wished for magic, some kind of Faustian exchange that would rewrite the laws of the universe and spin us forward, effortlessly leapfrogging the exhausting work of love. The outcome seemed so distant and theoretical. How did I know that this baby would become a girl and then a teenager and then, unthinkable, an adult—a woman? And what would that mean? That she would stay with me here onshore; or that we would fish together, she and I; or that she would be my younger self, and work side by side out on the water with Duncan? I didn't know.

Neither did I know then that she would be my only girl; that over the next fourteen years, there would be five more children—all boys. Had I known, would I have taught her differently, so that she would not scorn the kitchen or a life onshore, tending babies and gardens instead of wrestling saltwater and killing fish?

This summer, Naphtali turns seventeen. I don't know how many more summers she'll return to this island for fishing. I chose this life; she was born into it. The thought of being alone here on this island with all boys and men saddens me. When she leaves, what will she take with her? What do other mothers pass onto their daughters? Great-grandmother's china, Aunt Mary's handmade baskets, family recipes. I have none of these.

I want to give her something that is hers, and ours, alone; that cannot be given to my sons; that was not given to me. Something distinctly female that will ease and further her way down the path of womanhood. It has taken me a long time to become a woman out here; I had to find the way myself—a winding path between nursing babies, gutting fish, changing diapers, and spitting into storms. I wish its benefits and joys upon her much sooner than they came to me.

It is not fishing that I want to give. It was never really mine to bestow. That has always been her father's. And it is much more hers now than mine; it is already her lifelong work, even if she stops tomorrow. If she continues, she will have to sort out how to be a woman in this world and work, and decide how much it matters.

It's 7:45 PM, time to ready for the evening pick. Naphtali is going out with Emily, her best friend, who's here for a month working for me as a nanny. A respite from her usual company of men. Naphtali's bathroom ministrations for fishing usually mean a businesslike slathering of sunblock on her face, winding and pinning her hair up beneath a plastic shower cap then tying a bandana around it as protection from fish slime and blood. Her wardrobe: a thermal undershirt, sweatpants, wool socks pulled up over the ankles. Then the step into rubber hip boots, the pull of clownish orange-and-yellow bib rain pants, a foam lifejacket zippered over the top, vinyl gloves up to her forearms. All body shape erased.

This night, both girls emerge from the bathroom with the usual wardrobe but with their hair exposed, in ponytails, their faces transformed with rich red lipstick, huge hoop earrings, gypsy scarves, thick mascara and eye shadow. Laughing at this exaggeration of their own beauty, and laughing at where they will take it—out into the skiff, where gender is lost—they walk down the hill to the beach, their steps light with anticipation. Under her arm, Naphtali carries a digital camera and an unopened box of tampons. She has told me what they are up to. In honor of her birthday, they are designing their own digital cover of *Seventeen* magazine. They will feature an outhouse contest, a "fit-and-fabulous" exercise routine, and an article, set in the skiff, highlighting the tampons: "Menstruating in a Man's World." Out on the water, they take turns standing in the bow. Behind them, kelp dried on the skiff sides, fish at their feet—a backdrop to the glamour-girl smile at the camera, a finger pointing to the box of tampons on the knee.

It is just what mothers hope as they carry their newborn daughter home from the hospital—that their daughter will exceed them. She is stronger than I am—she is becoming a woman sooner than I did. I pray for her the courage to stay strong; the strength to keep singing when everyone else is silent. She has this already. More, I pray for her what she has not yet dared: the courage to be weak, the courage to ask for help, to cry when she needs to, to bleed when she must, to work beside men as a woman.

And most of all, if she cannot do this, for the courage to walk away. I will help her pack. And I will bear her absence—alone now in a world of fish and men—with all the strength of a woman.

Contributors

CAROLYN ALESSIO, a recovering suburbanite, lives with her family in Chicago. Her work appears in the Pushcart Prize anthology, TriQuarterly, *Boulevard*, and the *Chicago Tribune*.

BARBARA CARD ATKINSON is currently an associate editor at *Literary Mama* magazine. She has written for Salon, the *Christian Science Monitor*, and Brain,Child magazine. Her fiction is included in *Literary Mama: Reading for the Maternally Inclined*. She lives with her family in California.

JENNY BLOCK is a freelance writer and editor. She holds both her BA and her MA in English from Virginia Commonwealth University and is now working on her doctorate at the University of Virginia. For the past ten years, she has taught composition and rhetoric at the university level. Her most recent work includes two academic titles for the Newsweek Education Program, for which she also lectures at conferences across the country. Her writing has appeared in *Virginia Living* magazine, *Richmond* magazine, *Style Weekly* and *Literary Mama* magazine.

AMY BLOOM is the author of two short-story collections, a novel, and a book of essays. She has been nominated for the National Book Award and the National Book Critics Circle Award and has received the National Magazine Award for Fiction. She teaches at Yale.

GAYLE BRANDEIS is the author of Fruitflesh: Seeds of Inspiration for Women Who Write and The Book of Dead Birds: A Novel, which won Barbara Kingsolver's Bellwether Prize for Fiction in Support of a Literature of Social Change. She is a writer-in-residence for the Mission Inn Foundation's Family Voices Project and is on the faculty of the UCLA Writers' Program. She lives in Riverside, California, with her husband and two children. Her novel Self Storage will be published by Ballantine in 2007.

MARTHA BROCKENBROUGH writes an educational humor column for the award-winning online encyclopedia Encarta that is read annually by more than ten million people. She is author of It Could Happen to You: Diary of a Pregnancy and Beyond. She lives in Seattle with her husband, Adam Berliant, and their two girls.

ANDREA J. BUCHANAN is the author of Mother Shock: Loving Every (Other) Minute of It and managing editor of Literary Mama magazine. Her work has been featured in the Christian Science Monitor, Parents magazine, Nick Jr. magazine, and in the collections Breeder: Real-Life Stories from the New Generation of Mothers; Your Children Will Raise You: The Joys, Challenges, and Life Lessons of Motherhood; The Imperfect Mom: Candid Confessions of Mothers Living in the Real World; and About What Was Lost: 20 Writers on Miscarriage. In addition to editing the anthologies It's a Boy and It's a Girl, she is also the coeditor of *Literary Mama: Reading for the Maternally Inclined.* You can read more about her adventures in motherland at her website www.andibuchanan.com.

ANN DOUGLAS is the author of The Mother of All® Pregnancy Books, The Mother of All® Baby Books, and numerous other books about pregnancy and parenting. She writes the "Misconceptions" column for *Conceive* magazine and a pregnancy and motherhood column for CanadianLiving.com. She lives in Peterborough, Ontario, with her husband, Neil, and their four children. Ann's website can be found at www.having-a-baby.com.

LESLIE LEYLAND FIELDS teaches creative nonfiction in Seattle Pacific University's Master of Fine Arts program. She is the author of *Surprise Child, Surviving the Island of Grace, Out on the Deep Blue,* and *The Entangling Net.* Her essays have appeared in the *Atlantic, Orion, Best Essays Northwest, On Nature: Great Writers on the Great Outdoors,* and many other publications. For twenty-eight years she has lived on Kodiak Island, Alaska, where she commercial fishes each summer with her husband and six children. She can be reached at northernpen@alaska.com. Her author website is www.leslie-leyland-fields.com.

KIM FISCHER is a freelance writer specializing in grant proposals and fundraising materials for nonprofit organizations. She holds an MA and "ABD" in English from Temple University and has worked extensively as a university instructor and as a technical writer/trainer. She lives in Philadelphia with her husband and three daughters.

GWENDOLEN GROSS, dubbed "the reigning queen of women's adventure fiction" by *Book* magazine, is the author of *Field Guide* and *Getting Out*. She's won awards for her writing workshops, and she has published essays, poems, and stories in dozens of journals and anthologies of the more traditional variety—as well as those made with staples, feathers, Post-its, used popsicle sticks, googly eyes, and glitter, and whose editors are her son and daughter. She lives in northern New Jersey.

JESSICA BERGER GROSS graduated from Vassar College and received an MA in public policy from the University of Wisconsin-Madison. She is the editor of *About What Was Lost*, an anthology about miscarriage and pregnancy loss, and writes a column on yoga and health for *Yoga International* magazine. Jessica lives in Cambridge, Massachusetts, where she is teaching a class on memoir and the personal essay at the Harvard Extension School. She is also a columnist for *Literary Mama* magazine.

RACHEL HALL's essays and stories have appeared or are forthcoming in the anthologies *Mamaphonic*, *The Habit of Art*, and *About What Was Lost*. Her writing can also be found in a number of literary journals, including *Water~Stone*, the *Gettysburg Review*, and *New Letters*, which awarded her their 2004 Fiction Prize. She has received other honors and awards from *Lilith*, *Nimrod*, *Glimmer Train*, the Bread Loaf Writers' Conference, and the Constance Saltonstall Foundation for the Arts. She teaches creative writing and literature at the State University of New York-Geneseo, where she holds the Chancellor's Award for Excellence in Teaching.

KELLY H. JOHNSON is a former attorney turned freelance writer. She lives in Richmond, Virginia, with her husband and six children. He work has appeared in *Family Fun*, local parenting magazines, and the compilation *The Imperfect Mother*.

SUZANNE KAMATA left South Carolina in 1988 to teach English for a year in Japan and wound up staying. She now lives in Shikoku with her husband and bicultural twins. She is the editor of the anthology *The Broken Bridge: Fiction from Expatriates in Literary Japan* and the author of the forthcoming short-story collection *River of Dolls*. Her work has been nominated for the Pushcart Prize five times, and she is a two-time winner of the All Nippon Airways/Wingspan Fiction Contest. Her essays about being a mom have appeared in *Literary Mama* and *Brain,Child* magazines, the *Utne Reader*, *Skirt!*, and the *Japan Times*. She also contributed to the anthologies *Literary Mama: Reading for the Maternally Inclined* and *It's a Boy: Women Writers on Raising Sons*.

YVONNE LATTY is the author of *We Were There: Voices of African American Veterans from World War II to the War in Iraq*. A native of New York City, she earned a BFA in Film/Television and an MA in Journalism from New York University before becoming a reporter for the *Philadelphia Daily News*. She lives in Philadelphia with her family. You can visit Yvonne at www.yvonnelatty.com.

JENNIFER LAUCK is the author of three memoirs: *Blackbird: A Childhood Lost and Found*; *Still Waters*; and *Show Me the Way: A Memoir in Stories*, a collection of stories about mothering. She lives in Portland, Oregon, and is at work on a fourth memoir about being a mother and walking the spiritual path, as well as on a novel about the Virgin Mary. She also contributed to the anthologies *Literary Mama: Reading for the Maternally Inclined* and *It's a Boy: Women Writers on Raising Sons.*

JODY MACE is a freelance writer based in Charlotte, North Carolina, where she lives with her husband, Stan, and two children, Kyla and Charlie. In addition to writing, she works as a school librarian. Her work has appeared in many magazines, including *Family Circle, FamilyFun, Nick Jr.,* the *Christian Science Monitor,* and *Brain,Child,* as well as in the anthology *It's a Boy: Women Writers on Raising Sons.*

JENNIFER MARGULIS is the editor and coauthor of *Toddler: Real-Life Stories of Those Fickle, Irrational, Urgent, Tiny People We Love,* which won the Independent Book Publishers Association Award 2004 for the category "best parenting." A freelance writer, consultant, and photojournalist, she has published articles in *Ms.; Newsday; Pregnancy; Brain,Child; Parenting;* and dozens of other national and local publications. Her weekly column on parenting and life, "Tales from the Crib," appears on Mondays in the *Ashland Daily Tidings.* She is the creative nonfiction editor at *Literary Mama* magazine and her book *Why Babies Do That* was published in fall 2005. Jennifer lives in Ashland, Oregon, with her husband, two daughters, and one son.

JOYCE MAYNARD is the author of the bestselling memoir *At Home in the World* and five novels, including *To Die For* and *The Usual Rules,* named by the American Library Association one of the ten best novels for young readers in 2003. For eight years she authored the widely syndicated column "Domestic Affairs," about her experiences as a mother, and was a contributing editor and writer for Parenting magazine. A regular contributor to O magazine, MORE, and numerous other national publications, she is currently at work on Mirror, Mirror, a collection of women's stories about their bodies. Her new novel, to be published in paperback in June 2006, is The Cloud Chamber. The mother of three grown children, she makes her home in Mill Valley, California, and Lake Atitlán, Guatemala. Visit her on the web at www.JoyceMaynard.com.

JACQUELYN MITCHARD is the author of the New York Times best-selling novel The Deep End of the Ocean, which was chosen as the first book for Oprah Winfrey's Book Club. She has also written four other best-selling novels (The Most Wanted, A Theory of Relativity, Twelve Times Blessed, and Christmas, Present); an essay collection (The Rest of Us: Dispatches from the Mother Ship); two books of nonfiction (Mother Less Child: The Love Story of a Family and Jane Addams of Hull House); and two children's books (Starring Prima! and Baby Bat's Lullaby). Her latest books are the novel The Breakdown Lane and a children's book, Rosalie, My Rosalie: The Tale of a Duckling. Syndicated through Tribune Media Services, Mitchard writes a column that appears in 128 newspapers nationwide, and she is a contributing editor for Parenting magazine. Jacquelyn Mitchard lives near Madison, Wisconsin, with her husband, Christopher Brent, and their six children.

VICKY MLYNIEC's essays and articles have appeared in publications ranging from the Christian Science Monitor and the Washington Post to Redbook and Working Mother. She is also a short story writer who is the 2005 winner of the Tobias Wolff Award for Fiction and second-prize winner of the 2004 Baltimore Review Short Fiction competition. She grew up in the San Francisco Bay Area, earned her undergraduate degree from UC Berkeley in Slavic Languages and Literatures, and resides in the Santa Cruz Mountains with her husband and two sons.

CATHERINE NEWMAN is the author of the award-winning memoir *Waiting for Birdy: A Year of Frantic Tedium, Neurotic Angst, and the Wild Magic of Growing a Family* and of the child-raising journal "Bringing Up Ben & Birdy" on BabyCenter.com. She is a contributing editor for Family-Fun magazine, and her work has been published in numerous magazines and anthologies, including the *New York Times* best-selling *The Bitch in the House*, *Toddler*, and *It's a Boy: Women Writers on Raising Sons*. She lives in Massachusetts with her family.

MIRIAM PESKOWITZ is the author of *The Truth Behind the Mommy Wars: Who Decides What Makes a Good Mother* and speaks publicly about the cultural politics of motherhood. She is a mother, writer, and professor, and she has appeared on TV, radio, the Internet, and in print media throughout the country, including CNN, KQED's Forum with Michael Krasny, Seattle's KUOW and KCTS *Connects*, Philadelphia's *Radio Times* with Marty Moss-Coane, the *Atlantic Monthly*, and *Bitch* and *Bust* magazines. Visit her on the web at www.playgroundrevolution.com.

JILL SILER is the mother of two daughters. She lives in Miami Beach.

GABRIELLE SMITH-DLUHA is a freelance writer who also enjoys a position at Southern Oregon University advising students on studying abroad. She has taught English in Latin America and Europe with husband

and three children in tow. She has been an editor of works in translation from Czech to English, including *The Czech English Reader* and *English Idioms*.

REBECCA STEINITZ's essays and reviews have appeared in the *New Republic*, the *Utne Reader*, *Salon*, *Literary Mama*, *Hip Mama*, and the *Women's Review of Books*. In her other writing life, she has published numerous scholarly articles on nineteenth-century British diaries and fiction. She is currently a senior program officer at the American Academy of Arts and Sciences. She rides a battered blue bike.

EMILY ALEXANDER STRONG taught biology and ecology before becoming a mother of two daughters, Eliza and Harper. She began writing personal essays six years ago in response to the sudden death of her all-time favorite person, her brother John. She is currently training for her first triathlon and lives with her family in Ashland, Oregon.

SHARI MACDONALD STRONG is a freelance writer, editor, and marketing copywriter whose clients include a religious division of Random House. She is the author of several books, including *Oregon's Sanctuaries, Retreats, and Sacred Places*. Shari makes her home in Portland, Oregon, with her husband, photojournalist Craig Strong, and their children: six-year-old Eugenia, born in Russia, and three-year-old sons Will and Mac, born via gestational surrogacy.

KATHARINE WEBER is the author of the novels *Triangle*, *The Little Women*, *The Music Lesson*, and *Objects in Mirror Are Closer Than They Appear*. Visit her on the web at www.katharineweber.com.